Land of the Ascending Dragon
Rediscovering Vietnam

Land of the Ascending Dragon
Rediscovering Vietnam

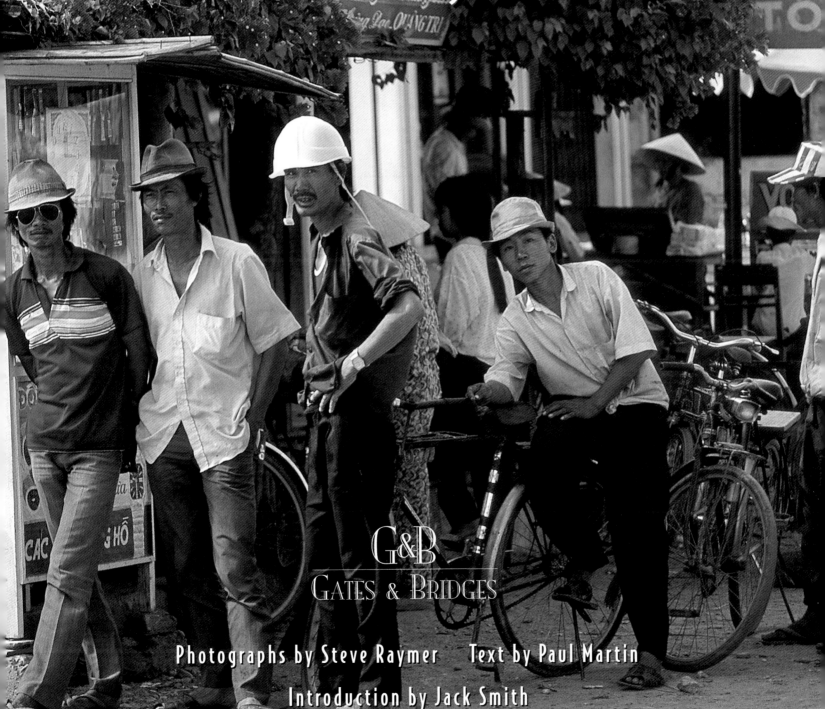

G&B
GATES & BRIDGES

Photographs by Steve Raymer   Text by Paul Martin

Introduction by Jack Smith

Fishermen rhythmically probe the depths of Hanoi's West Lake, or Lake of Mist. The lake has become a magnet for the capital's affluent, who have built luxurious waterside villas.

Page 1: Laden sampan motors along the Perfume River toward Hue, Vietnam's old imperial capital. Beyond rise slopes of the Truong Son Mountains, the rugged backbone of Vietnam.

Preceding pages: Vietnamese gather in the shade of bougainvillea at a bus stop at Quang Tri, a once thriving provincial capital along National Highway 1 that has yet to recover from being virtually leveled in 1972.

*Land of the Ascending Dragon
Rediscovering Vietnam*

Published by
Gates & Bridges
A Division of United Publishers Group, Inc.
50 Washington Street
Norwalk, Connecticut 06854

Photographs by
Steve Raymer

Text by
Paul Martin

Introduction by
Jack Smith

Produced by
Charles O. Hyman, Visual Communications, Inc.
   Washington, D.C.

Designed by
Kevin R. Osborn, Research & Design, Ltd.
   Arlington, Virginia

Photographs © 1997 by Steve Raymer
Text © 1997 by Paul Martin
Introduction © 1997 by Jack Smith
All rights reserved.

Library of Congress Catalog Number 97-071276

ISBN: 0-8038-9396-5

Distributed by Publishers Group West
Emeryville, California

Printed in Korea

10 9 8 7 6 5 4 3 2 1

Acknowledgments
The author and photographer would like to thank the following people for their assistance with this project: Alice Bishop, Joe Breen, John Brewer, Trevor Brown, David M. Burneston, Richard Busch, Ben Chapnick, Mercer Cross, Kevin Davis, Do Cong Minh, Do Hoai Giang, Melissa H. Driscoll, Wilbur E. Garrett, Robert Gray, Carolyn Wixson Haga, Sid Hastings, Steve Hettick, Bryan Hodgson, Bill Kimball, Ellen Kohlberg, K.M. Kostyal, Carol B. Lutyk, Janice Martin, Margaret Mendonca, Linda B. Meyerriecks, Salty O'Rourke, Pham Xuan Hoang An, Win Scudder, Robert B. Sims, Al Skinner, Barbara Skinner, Anh Stack, Dick Summers, Dick and Germaine Swanson, Joel Taubin, Tran Van Dinh, Vu Binh, the Freedom Forum, and the Vietnam travel specialists at Global Spectrum; Marcia Selva, Thuy M. Do, and Terry Abeles.

Credits
All black and white photographs courtesy of the National Archives of the United States, Washington, D.C., except the following: pages 9, 10, ABC News; pages 22, 35, Viet Nam News Agency; page 168, Agence France-Presse; pages 179, 180, Wilbur E. Garrett © National Geographic Society. Map, page 188, Susie Cooper. Index, Jim Enzinna.

THIS BOOK is dedicated to all those who shared in the Vietnam War experience, especially to those who made the ultimate sacrifice in that conflict. It is our hope that this volume will help open gates that have been too long closed, and offer a bridge to better understanding and goodwill between Americans and Vietnamese.

Contents

Woman tends terraced paddies in the lush Red River Delta beyond Hanoi. Agriculture engages some two-thirds of the country's labor force, with rice ever the most important crop.

A Vietnam Journey

by Jack Smith

ABC News Correspondent

I F VIETNAM had been a nuclear bomb, it could scarcely have had more impact on America. The war tore the country in two, poisoned politics and policy-making for years, and left deep wounds that still have not entirely healed. For those who fought in it, as I did, and for those who demonstrated against it, as some of my friends did, Vietnam remains the formative experience of a generation.

I went back there a few years ago, back to the killing fields in the Central Highlands where I nearly died. The experience was eye-opening. It changed me. Vietnam for me has started to become a place again, not a war. That's what this book is all about: letting go of the past, seeing Vietnam as it really is today—as a country, not a conflict.

For right or wrong, some three million Americans went off to serve in Vietnam; 58,000 of them were killed and another 153,000 were injured or crippled by bullets, shrapnel, or disease. But there were no parades for those who came home. Instead, they were rejected, pushed under the rug along with the unpopular and divisive war they served in. Vietnam veterans became bitter, angry, truly the lost Americans.

I was wounded. But I was lucky. I was not crippled, I am well employed, I have adjusted. However, for many years I shared the same bitterness as those veterans who were less fortunate than I toward the country that we all served so well and which afterward served us so poorly. It may sound silly, but veterans need a parade, some sort of public acceptance so they can put the war behind them and get on with life. Vietnam veterans never got that, and that's why so many of them for so long walked around carrying the war on their shoulders. A lot of Vietnam veterans never really left Vietnam, they never really came home.

I fought in one of the biggest and most vicious battles of the war, the Battle of the Ia Drang Valley. On the 17th of November 1965, a day that is burned into my memory, my battalion (about 500 men) was walking away from a place called Landing Zone X-Ray in South Vietnam's Central Highlands, a few miles from the Cambodian border. Along with other units of the 1st Air Cavalry Division, we had just fought in a major three-day battle there and had decisively defeated two regiments of the North Vietnamese Army. As we slipped through the jungle into another clearing, LZ Albany, we were jumped by a North Vietnamese formation. Like us, about 500-strong, and, like us, made up mostly of boys, 18 or 19 years old. But they had been in South Vietnam for a year, and so they were greatly more skilled at fighting and killing. Hearing us coming, they had quietly tied themselves up into the trees, uncoiled bandoliers of ammunition for their machine guns, snuck close in the chest-high razor grass.

Minutes after the guns opened up, we 500 were overwhelmed and fighting for our lives. Men rolled in the grass and stabbed at each other, gouged and punched, or blazed away at enemy soldiers just a few feet from them. I was lying so close to a North Vietnamese machine-gunner that I simply reached out and stuck my rifle into his face, pulled the trigger, and blew his head off.

At one point in that awful afternoon as my battalion was being cut to pieces, a small group of enemy came upon me, and thinking I had been killed (I was covered with other people's blood), proceeded to use me as a sandbag for their machine gun. I closed my eyes and pretended to be dead. I remember the gunner had bony knees that pressed against my sides. He didn't discover I was alive because he was trembling more than I was. He was, like me, just a teenager. The gunner began firing into the remnants of my company. My buddies began firing back with rifle grenades. I remember thinking, "Oh, my God, if I stand up the North Vietnamese will kill me and if I stay lying down my buddies will get me...." Before I went completely mad, a volley of grenades exploded all around and on top of me, killing the enemy boy and injuring me.

It went on like this all day and much of the night. I was wounded twice and thought myself dead. My company suffered 93 percent casualties. I watched all the friends I had in the world die. It is not the sort of thing you forget. The battlefield was covered with blood and littered with body parts, and it reeked of gunpowder and vomit. I discovered with a shock, as other soldiers have, that the only thing separating me from meat hanging in a butcher's shop was a thin piece of skin.

Twenty-year-old Pvt. Jack Smith shortly before the Battle of the Ia Drang Valley, which took place in November 1965.

This sort of experience leaves scars. I had nightmares, and for years afterward I was sour on life, by turns angry, cynical, and alienated.

Then one day I woke up and saw the world as I believe it really is, a bright and warm place. I looked afresh at my scars and marveled, not at the frailty of human flesh, my flesh, but at the indomitable strength of the human spirit. In spite of bullets, in spite of hot metal fragments, the spirit lives on. This is the miracle of life. Like other Vietnam veterans, I began to put my personal hurt behind me and started to examine the war itself.

When I went back to Vietnam a few years ago, I met Gen. Vo Nguyen Giap, the man who engineered the defeat of the French at Dien Bien Phu and then commanded North Vietnamese forces in the war with South Vietnam (and us). He conceded that because of the Ia Drang his plan to cut Vietnam in half and take the capital was delayed by ten years. "But," he chuckled, "it didn't make a difference, did it?"

We Americans won every battle, but the North Vietnamese, in the end, took Saigon. What on earth had we been doing there? Was all that pain and suffering worth it, or was it just a terrible waste? This is why Vietnam veterans don't really let go, why many can't get on with their lives, what sets them apart from veterans of other wars.

Nothing is so precious to a nation as its youth. And so, to squander the lives of the young in a war that, depending on one's point of view, either should never have been fought, or we were never prepared to win, seems crazy. Yet, that's exactly what happened in Vietnam. However justified the war seemed in 1964 and 1965 (and, remember, almost all Americans then thought it was), it no longer seemed that way after 1968. And no matter what you may remember of the war, we never really fought it to win.

When I was wounded it caused a minor sensation at home. My father is Howard K. Smith, the anchorman and TV commentator, who was then at the peak of his career. That the son of a famous person should get shot in Vietnam was, in 1965, news. When I returned to the U.S., President Johnson (who was a friend of my father's) invited me to a dinner party at the White House. I remember a tall, smiling man who thanked me for my service and sacrifice. I liked him then, I still do today. Yet, no one bears as much responsibility for the conduct of the war as he.

Aftermath of the Battle of the Ia Drang Valley, one of the war's fiercest actions, in which over 200 Americans died.

Nothing is so drastic as war. If one is going to fight, fight all out. But in Vietnam, we were never totally committed. And led by Lyndon Johnson—one of the country's best domestic presidents, but in foreign affairs, one of its most naive—we escalated piecemeal (in the Gulf we took six months to put half a million troops in the war zone; in Vietnam, more than six years). We were too timid to carry the fight to the enemy until the end, and we tried to keep the war contained to South Vietnam.

The result was that our enemy, a small country waging total war (i.e., using all its resources), saw a superpower fighting a limited war, and concluded that if it could just sustain the 10-to-1 casualties we were inflicting for a while (after all, North Vietnam produced babies faster than we could kill its soldiers), then we would tire and leave, and it would win. Of course, Ho Chi Minh was right. It worked with the French, and it worked later with the United States. After the Tet Offensive in 1968 we quit and began the longest and costliest retreat in U.S. history. Dean Rusk, the then-Secretary of State, many years later ruefully told me, "They outlasted us." The fact is, democracies don't fight inconclusive wars for remote goals in distant places for very long.

Lyndon Johnson harnessed his generals to a basically civilian policy—fighting the war piecemeal in the vain hope that no one in the U.S. would notice. As for the enemy, he treated Ho Chi Minh like a member of the congressional opposition: Show him the U.S. was tougher, and he'd give up. But Ho saw the incrementalism that resulted as a sign of weakness and hung on. Tens of thousands of young Americans died needlessly.

Whether the war was right or wrong, it was fought in such a way that it could never have been brought to a conclusion. That now seems clear with time. What a waste. It's why so many veterans of Vietnam feel bitter.

Well, we finally did get our parades, and we finally did build our memorial on the Mall in Washington. These helped. But so many veterans were still haunted by the war, and I was, too.

Seven years ago, I watched the Berlin Wall come down, and, as an ABC News correspondent, I witnessed firsthand on a number of trips the collapse of Communism. The policy of containment worked! We won the Cold War. And however meaningless Vietnam seemed at the time, it contributed to the fall of Communism. That was something to hold onto. Pretty thin and not very satisfying as a justification for what I and some of my friends went through in Vietnam. But at least it was something.

Then three years ago came an event that changed me—an opportunity to go back to Vietnam for ABC. With ten other Ia Drang veterans I traveled back to the jungle in the Central Highlands and walked the Ia Drang battlefield for several days in the company of some of the North Vietnamese we had fought against 30 years before. Did I find the answer to my question about the futility of the war? No, I don't know if what I and the rest of us did in the war was worth it. But what I did find surprised me.

North Vietnam may have conquered the South, but it is losing the peace. A country that two decades ago had the fourth strongest army in the world, has squandered its wealth on quarreling with and fighting most of its neighbors and is poor and bankrupt as a result. Vietnam today is stumbling towards capitalism, and Communism there is dying.

More important, much more important, Vietnam is a country profoundly at peace. Because the North Vietnamese feel they won, they are not haunted by the same ghosts as we. Arriving in Hanoi and spending some time in the north before going south, our group was made profoundly aware of this. The memorials and cemeteries that dot the countryside, to most people we met, were just artifacts from another time. And people could not understand what our little group of gray-haired, middle-aged Americans was doing there, what demons we were trying to exorcise, because they didn't have those demons.

Even in the south, most people were born after the war, and don't care much about it. We discovered that English is being taught again and is becoming the second language. Children delighted in practicing their schoolroom knowledge on us. People waved and smiled. They liked us. As we traveled around in a bus gawking at the rice paddies, we felt safe in a country where before fear had been our constant companion.

What struck me was the overwhelming peacefulness of the place, even in the clearing where I had fought. We helicoptered out to it for an emotional day's walk through the scrub jungle and tall grass where we had left the innocence of our youth behind. I broke down several times. I wanted to bring back some shrapnel, or shell casings, some physical manifestation of the battle to lay at the wall of the Vietnam Veterans Memorial in Washington, under the black granite of panel number three, where all my army buddies' names are carved, more than 200 of them. But, do you know, search as I did, I could not find any battle debris. The force of nature had simply erased it. And where once the grass had been slippery with blood, there were flowers blooming in that place of death. It was beautiful and still, and so I pressed some flowers and brought them back to lay at the foot of panel number three at the Vietnam Memorial. That is all that I could find in that jungle clearing that once held terror, and now held beauty.

To come to terms with Vietnam means ultimately letting go—to make Vietnam become a place again, and not a war, as it still is, unfortunately, for many of my fellow veterans. What I discovered in Vietnam may seem obvious, but it had really escaped me all those years on my journey away from Vietnam: The war is over. It certainly is for Vietnam and the Vietnamese. As I said on a *Nightline* broadcast when I came home, "This land is at peace, and so should we be." For me, Vietnam has become a place again, not a war, and I have begun letting go.

That's what this book is all about: Vietnam as a place, again, not a war. It is a great book. Enjoy it. Peace.

CHAPTER 1

City of the Soaring Dragon:
Hanoi

THE INTERCOM in the Hong Kong airport departure lounge kept blaring messages in English and Chinese as the minutes ticked away toward my 4:55 p.m. flight to Hanoi. It was still hard for me to believe I was returning to Vietnam, where I'd served as a Navy journalist in 1970-71. Once, I'd vowed to never again set foot in that green apostrophe of land so few Americans had ever heard of before the 1960s. I'd been a reluctant participant in the war, serving more out of a Sunday-school-and-Boy-Scout-bred sense of obligation than from any heartfelt belief in our cause. And I'd nearly been killed by a Viet Cong rocket. So why did I want to go back, after two dozen years?

Quite simply, I wanted to see the Vietnam that I'd missed the first time. Over the years, I'd become embarrassed by how little I knew about this place that had been such a central experience in my life. Now I wanted to see it all: a thousand-mile-long country that is slightly larger than Italy, a nation of vibrant cities and myriad cultural treasures, a land as beautiful as any in the world, with mist-wreathed mountains rolling down to the indigo South China Sea and mysterious temples enshrouded in vines and centuries. I wanted to survey the rumpled Truong Son Range, which runs nearly the length of Vietnam; the pristine beaches and quiet coastal lagoons; and those lush-beyond-imagining rice fields that stretch from the Red River Delta in the north to the Mekong Delta in the south. And yes, I wanted to revisit the places where I'd served long ago, to gauge what power they still held over me.

What I would discover on my journey from Hanoi to Ho Chi Minh City was a 2,000-year-old country reinventing itself at a furious pace, leaping from the early 20th-century

Too young to remember wars with France and the United States, smartly dressed youths on a Hanoi street symbolize the success of a fledgling free-market economy. Vietnam's move toward capitalism in 1986 signaled an effort to catch up with the country's more prosperous Asian neighbors.

infrastructure imposed by decades of war and
economic isolation directly into the 21st-century
world of computers and cellular phones. I would
find a remarkably youthful country—nearly half
the 75 million Vietnamese now living were born
since 1975. What I would not encounter was a single
citizen who showed the slightest animosity toward
me on learning that I was an American.

I looked around at the other passengers waiting
to board Vietnam Airlines Flight 791. Most were
Asian travelers, an assortment of kids and parents
and old people, clutching their parcels and carry-ons.
There were also many businessmen, their briefcases
bulging with schemes to bring the world to Vietnam.
Now that Vietnam's Communist leaders have relaxed
the ham-fisted grip of central planning, foreign
investors are eager to jump into the country's free-
wheeling economy, with Taiwan, Japan, Singapore,
Hong Kong, and South Korea up at the head of
the line.

The few non-Asians around me were
mostly French-speaking travelers—returning to
L'Indochine, the one-time colony over which the
French had held sway for nearly a hundred years,
from 1859, when they seized Saigon, until their
Indochinese empire came tumbling down on the battlefield at Dien Bien Phu, in 1954. In the eight-year
war leading to their ouster from Vietnam, the French
lost more than 35,000 men to the Communist Viet
Minh. I felt a strange kinship with these French
families, the slender couples in their fashionable
European attire, their tanned, good-looking children
around them. Though both our nations had been
losers in Vietnam, we were being drawn back to that
country that had so angrily repulsed us. It was difficult to let go of Vietnam. "Namstalgia," somebody
called it.

Then suddenly our boarding call came. The
shiny white Vietnam Airlines jet with the blue
flying-stork logo stood out sharply against the
green Hong Kong hills. It was a relief to know that
we were traveling on one of the new Airbuses that are

*Protected by earthen dikes that hold back
the muddy Red River, decrepit and often
gray Hanoi shows signs of a resurgence
after years of postwar depression. New
hotels, restaurants, and karaoke bars are
springing up along the capital's wide,
tree-lined boulevards.*

Street markets in Hanoi's Old Quarter burst into bloom during Tet, the annual celebration of the lunar new year. Many Vietnamese buy plum blossom sprigs and take them home to decorate for the country's biggest holiday, which falls in late January or early February.

replacing Vietnam's aging fleet of Soviet airliners.

Trooping up the boarding stairway, I got my first rush of déjà vu. Standing just inside the doorway were two pretty Vietnamese stewardesses, dressed in pink *ao dai* over white silk trousers. The young women were smiling demurely, their black hair gleaming like moonlit water. They were daughters of the generation that was young when I first went to Vietnam. I felt myself goggling at these delicate creatures just as I'd done as a 24-year-old serviceman arriving in Saigon. History books would have us believe that the French tried to cling to their Indochinese colony for its wealth of natural resources, but I know the real reason. To see a lithe beauty like these strolling along the boulevard, her hair spilling down her back, the

tails of her ao dai floating on the breeze—well....

I found my seat and settled in next to an older Asian couple, a dignified gray-haired gentleman in a jacket and tie and a pleasant-looking woman I took to be his wife. As the plane started taxiing toward the runway, I pulled out my Vietnamese phrase book and renewed my attempt to master a few basic expressions: Hello, *Chao;* Excuse me, *Xin loi;* Thank you, *Cam on;* My name is..., *Ten toi la....*

The gentleman next to me smiled as he saw me mouthing the words. "You are learning to speak Vietnamese?" he inquired politely.

"Trying," I said, closing my book. "Are you Vietnamese?"

The man nodded.

"You live in Hanoi?"

"Houston."

"Just visiting?"

"I will be visiting my sister and brother." A far-away look came over the man's face. "I have not seen them since 1948."

P.D. Nguyen, I learned, was a physician who'd been born in Hanoi. His family had become separated during the war against the French. He'd ended up living in Saigon after 1954, when the country was partitioned into the Communist North and the non-Communist South by the Geneva Accords, the negotiated settlement of the Franco-Viet Minh War. When the country was divided, nearly a million people—most of them Catholics—had migrated south, leaving behind everything to escape living under Communism. The Geneva Accords had called for nationwide elections in 1956, but those never happened: The South's provisional ruler, Ngo Dinh Diem, feared a victory by Ho Chi Minh. Diem held a referendum on his continued rule, afterward proclaiming himself president of a new Republic of Vietnam. America immediately recognized the Diem regime. The U.S. closed its consulate in Hanoi in December 1955 and would have no diplomatic relations with the North for the next 40 years.

Dr. Nguyen had left for America in 1975, along with his wife. She had never met his Hanoi relatives.

"Will you be staying with them?"

Dr. Nguyen nodded. I detected a wan smile. "We would be more comfortable in a hotel—their house is...rather old—but that would hurt them."

The jet swept down the runway and lifted off. Slowly, the hills of Hong Kong dropped away beneath us, the high rises and ship-filled harbor receding below a skein of clouds.

Less than two hours later we were descending over the verdant landscape outside Hanoi. I looked down on the green humps of hills and board-flat expanses, wondering if perhaps my brother-in-law, a Navy pilot during the war, might have flown over this very stretch of ground on the way to his bombing targets. Dr. and Mrs. Nguyen were both staring

fixedly out the window. Then the tires of the airliner met the asphalt with a shriek, and the jet engines were reversing thrust, throwing us against our seat belts. The engines seemed to build to a thunderous fanfare: Viet…*NAM!*

I grabbed my carry-on bag from the overhead compartment and wished Dr. and Mrs. Nguyen good luck. Emerging into the soft, warm Vietnamese air, I felt an emotion I hadn't expected: a strange sense of homecoming—I owned a little piece of Vietnam, just as it owned a piece of me, and I was returning to inspect my claim.

Daylight was fading fast. The landscape around Noi Bai Airport was a minimalist scene of open spaces, with only a few low buildings some distance away. We had literally landed in the middle of nowhere—the airport is about a 45-minute drive north of the capital. I was struck once again by the fecundity of the countryside, an intensity of green to make even Ireland's famous landscape pale in comparison. Everything was stilled by a settling mist. The smells were the familiar damp, rotting-plant odors of the tropics, underlaid with jet fumes.

In a relatively short while—after a poker-faced immigration officer had stamped my papers, and my bags had been passed through an ancient x-ray machine resembling a small atomic reactor—I was launched into the humid night in the Socialist Republic of Vietnam. Outside the terminal stood a gesticulating wall of Vietnamese taxi drivers, all wanting to snag me as a fare. Among them I spotted a thin young man holding a placard with my name on it.

"Mr. Paul Martin?"

The young man held out his hand. "I am your guide, Giang." He was wearing jeans and a long-sleeve black shirt casually rolled up to the elbows. His short black hair, combed straight back, was wavy, a rarity among Vietnamese. I would come to learn that Do Hoai Giang was the 22-year-old son of a father who teaches Russian and speaks seven languages, and a mother who is a guide for French-speaking tour groups; Giang himself had studied Russian for six

years, including a year in Moscow. I would also find out that the young man's non-Vietnamese-looking hair and eyes had caused him grief as a boy in his race-conscious country: "Other children, they said I am not Vietnamese. I hit them." Even as an adult, Giang would tell me, he was often mistaken for a Japanese tourist.

Giang ushered me through the crowd to a late model Toyota. Tung, the driver, was a relentlessly grinning man with an abundance of teeth and a long lock of hair he had to continuously swipe away from his eyes. It was dark when we pulled away from the airport—and in the Vietnamese countryside, darkness is serious stuff. No streetlights, no lighted commercial buildings along the road. The ride into Hanoi was like a trip through a coal mine, with only

your helmet beam to show the way. Figures hove into view now and then, caught in the glare of the Toyota's headlights—pedestrians, bicyclists, people on motorbikes. They danced and flickered away in an instant as we passed by, like figures in a home movie. We passed occasional shanties with naked light bulbs dangling inside; the weak orange illumination those bulbs threw off was sucked into the blackness two feet beyond the huts' open doors.

As we neared Hanoi we crossed the Red River, though I never saw it in the dark. We were driving along the arm of land lying between the dike that holds the Red River in check during monsoon season and the body of water called West Lake—the Lake of Mist. With a circumference of eight miles, West Lake is the largest of the network of lakes that

Hanoi residents dressed in period costumes parade to Dong Da Hill, site of a 1789 victory over Chinese invaders by Vietnamese hero Nguyen Hue. A millennium of Chinese rule (111 B.C.- A.D. 938) and periodic wars against China have greatly influenced Vietnamese culture.

Young woman sells hand-painted masks on Paper Street in Hanoi's Old Quarter. Since the 15th century, the so-called 36 Streets of the Old Quarter have borne names such as Gold Street, Silk Street, and Broiled Fish Street, reflecting the items traditionally sold along them.

Camera mounted beneath an Air Force fighter-bomber catches its deadly payload in midstream. Called Operation Rolling Thunder, the sustained bombing of North Vietnam by U.S. Air Force, Navy, and Marine Corps warplanes began in March 1965.

Clouds of black smoke billow from an oil storage area on the outskirts of Hanoi after it was bombed in June 1966. A total of 922 U.S. aircraft were lost over North Vietnam between 1965 and 1968, when the bombing was halted by President Lyndon Johnson. President Richard Nixon resumed aerial attacks against Hanoi in 1972.

spangle this city of 2.5 million souls like a handful of glinting coins tossed on a tabletop.

The ambient light from shops and homes cast a pale orange glow on the road. We passed occasional villas built by the city's nouveaux riches. Here on the outskirts of the city, the traffic was becoming increasingly thicker. All around was the constant roar of motorbikes, like the drone of some colossal insect. An American driver would have considered himself hopelessly stuck in this rattling mass of vehicles, but somehow our Toyota kept forging ahead, Tung working his horn hard.

We skirted the eastern edge of Hanoi's Old Quarter, the main commercial district, fronting the Red River just south of West Lake. The familiar architecture of the tropics closed in around us, a warren of low, boxy stucco shops little wider than a car, their collapsible steel security gates pushed to the sides. The buildings were painted mostly yellow or white, though dirt and mildew had mellowed them into a universal dun color.

I was staying in one of the capital's new hotels just south of the Old Quarter, in the central district of Hoan Kiem. The French called this part of the city Ville Française. It's the modern heart of the capital. The best hotels and stores are here, as are many embassies, situated in some of the colonial-era buildings of ocher stucco that give Hanoi the feel of being caught in a time warp. Hoan Kiem's wide, tree-lined boulevards evoke the days when Hanoi was the Paris of the North. From 1902 until 1953, the French lavished their best landscaping and architecture on the city, capital of their Indochinese empire.

Tung pulled up in front of a modern, glass-fronted building, the Thuy Tien Hotel. Inside was a lobby done up in Vietnamese modern: everything well lit and glittering—glass and tile and polished wood, accented with numerous potted plants. American easy-listening music drifted from the dining room/bar at the end of the lobby. Behind the check-in counter stood three young women in ao dai of yellow, pink, and blue, their long hair tied back in

ponytails. They were giggling and whispering to each other, like brightly colored birds twittering in the branches of a tree.

The second-floor room I was shown to was clean and spartan, with a veranda overlooking the street. On TV, I could choose among the BBC, India's Channel "V"—featuring nonstop MTV-like videos (rapping Hindus in turbans!)—or local Vietnamese programming (I would watch one war movie in which American fighter pilots were portrayed with wonderfully hammy villainy by Vietnamese actors).

I helped myself to a cold 333-brand beer from the refrigerator and pulled a chair onto the veranda. Lighting a cigar, I put my feet up on the wrought-iron railing. The night air was pleasantly warm, and the sounds of the city were curiously familiar: sputtering motorbikes and barking dogs...shouting children at play, the tinny whir of air conditioners. Down in the dimly lit street, bicyclists passed the hotel at a leisurely pace. (Riding around aimlessly of an evening is one of the chief entertainments here, since most people are living on top of one another in shoe-box apartments.) A householder just up the way dumped a pail of vegetable scraps along the curb for the late night garbage collectors—old women who trundle around the deserted streets pushing tin garbage cans mounted on wheels, scooping up refuse with brushes and pans. On the ground floor of the building across from me, a woman inside a beauty parlor was having her hair washed.

Life went on apace in Hanoi.

I sent a stream of cigar smoke into the air. Here I sat, a Yankee in the capital of one of the last bastions of Communism, smoking a Cuban cigar a friend had given me and sipping a beer that owed its name to the former French colonizers of Vietnam. Just as I was about to draw some profound conclusion from all that, I was spotted by a spiky-haired toddler on the veranda of an apartment on the opposite side of the street. He waved cheerily and shouted "Hi" at least a dozen times.

Close to ground zero, Kham Thien Street, near the Hanoi Railway Station, was leveled by U.S. bombers on December 26, 1972. Today the street pulses with traffic and well-stocked shops that sell everything from videos of American movies to Western pharmaceuticals and fashions. Remembering a friend from the war years, an elderly resident of Kham Thien Street (opposite) is consumed with grief.

GHOSTS OF HANOI PAST

Beyond the open window of the hotel restaurant, the city was coming to life. People methodically swept the sidewalks in front of their homes or shops. Street vendors were setting up along the curb. Vegetable peddlers shuffled past with baskets of produce dangling from poles across their shoulders. An arm's length from my breakfast table, school kids walked by in clean white shirts or blouses, the older girls virginal in all-white ao dai. Nearly all Vietnamese children receive at least a primary education, producing a remarkable literacy rate of around 90 percent. But even for the country's highly educated young, too few jobs exist, and the per capita income barely tops $300 a year, ranking Vietnam among the poorest nations on earth.

Giang showed up punctually at eight o'clock, and we set off for the sight that for me—and countless other Americans—is the painful symbol of this city: the infamous "Hanoi Hilton." It was a pilgrimage I had to make, though not one I expected to enjoy. Tung deftly negotiated the morning rush of bicycles and motorbikes on the way to the former prison, a short distance away near the center of town. Looking beyond all the blue-and-gold signs advertising Tiger Beer and the red political banners suspended between trees, I found my initial impressions of the night before reconfirmed: Vietnam's capital was a jumble of Third World scruffiness relieved by the greenery of frequent parks and occasional pockets of opulence, such as the city's grandiose Municipal Theatre, built in 1911 in the baroque style of the

Paris Opera House, and the starched-white Metropole, the longtime queen of Hanoi lodgings. All around the skyline, construction cranes loomed as new hotels were shooting up like bamboo.

The complex known as the Hanoi Hilton—officially Hoa Lo Prison—had been built by the French early in this century. Occupying a whole city block, it was a dank, depressing place of no escape, enclosed by walls of mildewing yellow plaster four feet thick and 20 feet high. At one time the prison housed over 700 American POWs, some incarcerated for seven years or more. The lucky souls who survived here were given their freedom in March 1973, after being fattened up, allowed to bathe, and issued clean clothes for the first time in years.

Tung parked across the street from the old

prison, and Giang and I approached those dirty yellow walls, which turned out to be nearly all that remained of the structure. Sunlight poured into the gutted interior, where only a couple of rooms in a far corner were still standing. The compound was being demolished to make way for a new hotel and office complex, with a small museum to document the history of Hoa Lo Prison.

I stood near the front gate, watching workmen root around in the piles of rubble to which this unhappy place had been reduced. For an instant I thought about picking up one of the bricks lying about as a souvenir, but then it struck me that such an act would be a sacrilege to the memory of those who'd suffered here, on the order of carting home a piece of a Nazi concentration camp to display on

your mantle. Better to leave that sort of symbol where it lay.

I must have lingered too long watching the workmen, for a stern-looking fellow came over to ask what I was doing. Giang turned back toward the car. "Time to go," he said simply.

A few minutes later, I stood gazing at a historical marker beside Truc Bach Lake, a short ride north of downtown near West Lake. The silver plaque noted that U.S. Navy pilot John McCain—today's Arizona senator—had parachuted into Truc Bach Lake in 1967 after ejecting from his downed Skyhawk. The image of someone wafting down into a lake in the middle of a populous city would have been comical had I not known that McCain, son of a senior Navy admiral, had spent the next five and a half years as a POW, surviving a broken knee and two broken arms from his crash, followed by countless rounds of torture.

As an American, it would have been easy for me to latch onto such reminders of our past connection with Vietnam, to fixate on the negative. Fortunately, I had the example of Senator McCain himself to emulate. That man who endured so much suffering in this very city had been a leader in advocating a return to normalcy in our relations with the Vietnamese—in seeking to put the past behind us and move on.

Back in central Hanoi, I moved on to the task of unraveling something of Vietnam's lengthy heritage. The city's highly regarded History Museum preserves the record of Vietnam from its beginnings in prehistory up until the year 1945. (To get the story of the country from 1945 to the present, you have to visit the Museum of the Revolution.) The History Museum occupies a handsome green-roofed building of pale orange stucco, fancied up with Oriental flourishes around its windows—the French School of the Far East in an earlier incarnation. When the History Museum opened in 1933, its collection covered all of Southeast Asia. After the Vietnamese regained control of their country in 1954, the focus was narrowed to Vietnam. I paid my admission fee and, for a few extra dollars, hired an English-speaking guide, a cordial, gray-haired gentleman who helped make sense of the wealth of artifacts displayed on the museum's two floors.

As I followed him through the airy, high-ceilinged rooms, the guide kept up a steady patter, deluging me with facts and dates. Led past glass cases containing Paleolithic and Neolithic stone tools discovered in Vietnam, I got the message that this locale has been inhabited for quite some time. Vietnam's Bronze Age Dong Son culture left behind wonderfully wrought bronze funeral urns and ceremonial drums, among other artifacts. The guide pointed out a 2,500-year-old urn decorated with figures of couples making love. "This means 'life goes on,'" he explained. We walked past a row of barrel-size ceremonial drums decorated with scenes of everyday life: people playing musical instruments or flailing rice. The drums supposedly could reach the ears of the faithful a kilometer away. There were also 2,000-year-old bronze statuettes that looked remarkably like Inca figures.

According to legend, the first king of the Vietnamese was Lac Long Quang. To make peace with the Chinese, he is said to have married Au Co, a Chinese immortal. Au Co bore Lac Long Quang one hundred sons, hatched from a hundred eggs. Eventually the king and queen separated. The queen took 50 sons to live in the mountains, the king and the other 50 sons remaining to rule the lowlands.

This fanciful story has at least some basis in Vietnamese history (see pages 186-187 for an overview of Vietnam's history and an accompanying chronology). The fate of the early Vietnamese was tied to the Chinese, who ruled over the Red River Delta for a thousand years, from 111 B.C. to A.D. 938. During that time, the Chinese introduced the Vietnamese to aspects of rice cultivation—the metal plow, domesticated water buffaloes, and dikes for irrigation—still in use today. The Chinese also passed on their philosophy and religions: Confucianism,

Taoism, and Buddhism. The Vietnamese would even adopt Chinese ideograms for writing, though around the 13th century they adapted the characters to their own system. (Vietnam's present Latin-based script was devised by a 17th-century French Jesuit scholar, Alexandre de Rhodes.)

The History Museum's most engrossing display was the one that documented the Vietnamese defeat of the Mongol horde of Kublai Khan. Three times—

in 1257, 1284, and 1287—the Mongols invaded Vietnam, with armies of up to half a million men. Each time they were rebuffed by Vietnam's legendary Tran Hung Dao. The final time the Mongols attacked, they came by sea rather than overland. Using light vessels to harry their foes, Tran Hung Dao's forces lured the deeper-draft Mongol vessels up the Bach Dang River, where the Vietnamese had planted sharpened stakes underwater. The Mongol ships were impaled on the stakes, sinking a thousand vessels. The museum possesses some of the original stakes used by the defenders, and five are on display near a mural depicting the battle.

I thanked my genial guide for the tour as he walked me to the front door, urging me to come back sometime. Outside, the late morning sun was trying

Old Quarter vendor in a traditional conical hat sells the latest millinery. The warren of narrow streets, merchants' stalls, and sidewalk restaurants that make up the Old Quarter (above) began as a collection of villages surrounding the palace of Emperor Ly Thai Tong, who moved his capital here in 1010, making Hanoi one of Asia's oldest cities.

Pages 24-25: Worshipers jam Hanoi's Ambassadors' (or Quan Su) Pagoda on Wandering Souls Day, an important Buddhist holiday. In the 17th century, the shrine was the site of a guesthouse for ambassadors of Buddhist countries. Vietnam's all-powerful Communist government has lifted some restrictions on religious freedom, but the clergy of all faiths remain closely monitored.

unsuccessfully to burn through the perpetually gray skies that hover over the northern part of the country during the chilly, drizzly winter and early spring, though now, in mid-April, Hanoi was enjoying highs in the 70s. "Hanoi's weather is better than Ho Chi Minh City's," Giang would inform me, in one of his frequent demonstrations of northern chauvinism. "We have four seasons," he explained, "they only have two—hot and rainy."

Serenade among the Sages

Just a few blocks west of the Old Quarter is one of Vietnam's architectural treasures, the Temple of Literature. Founded in the year 1070, the walled complex of buildings honors Confucius, whose works have influenced the Vietnamese for 2,000 years. In 1076, the temple grounds became the site of the country's first university. From here arose the ruling class of Vietnam, the mandarins who shone in mathematics, poetry, philosophy, finance, and statesmanship.

Visitors enter the temple through the Great Portico, a two-story stone gate flanked by carvings of an ascending dragon—Vietnamese symbol of good luck—and a tiger, representing strength. An inscription on the gate modestly proclaims, "Among the

Vietnam's capitalist bandwagon beckons a curbside vendor in Hanoi. But name-brand televisions stamped "Made in Vietnam" are beyond the reach of many Vietnamese. With a per capita income of about $300 a year, Vietnam ranks with Bangladesh as one of the world's poorest countries.

Signs of the times: An executive scurries around Hanoi in a pedicab, or cyclo. International businessmen must battle the country's labyrinthine and often corrupt bureaucracy. Hanoi's trade with the West began in 1626 with the arrival of a Dutch merchant ship, and by the 18th century the city had become a busy trading port.

Performer brightens Hanoi's nearly thousand-year-old Temple of Literature. Vietnam's first university, the temple was where the children of early emperors and high-ranking officials were educated in Confucian thought and behavior. With its traditional architecture, the temple presents a favored location for filmmakers.

Imposing statue of Vladimir I. Lenin, founder of the Soviet Union, stands tucked away in Chi Long Park on Hanoi's Dien Bien Phu Street. While most young Vietnamese eschew politics in favor of careers and making money, their country remains one of the last Communist states in the world, along with China, North Korea, and Cuba.

doctrines of the world, ours is best, and is revered by all culture-starved lands." Just outside the gate, two stone stelae command all who enter to dismount from their horses; even the king was included, a sign that knowledge was held in higher regard than royalty.

Within the compound are six acres of shady, parklike grounds. Brick paths lined with carefully tended shrubbery led me beneath banyan and frangipani trees, past lotus ponds and pavilions with gracefully curving tile roofs. Few other visitors were about, though some young Vietnamese were sketching the temple's ornate architecture. Students still come here to pray for good luck in their exams.

Interior walls divide the compound into five courtyards, linked by walkways representing the scholar's path to knowledge. The third courtyard is

the most interesting. Beneath tile-roofed pavilions on either side of a large central pond—the Well of Heavenly Clarity—82 great round stone tortoises bear tall tablets that record the names and villages of the 1,306 scholars who earned doctorates from the university between 1442 and 1779. Those gaining this distinction ranged in age from 16 to 61—evidence that both the precocious and the late bloomer were represented at the university.

This honor roll in stone was meant to pay permanent tribute to the nation's men of learning, but by the late 18th century the original pavilions that sheltered the stelae had gone to ruin, and the tablets were scattered. During the Vietnam War, the stelae were buried in sand and surrounded by a thick concrete wall to protect them from U.S. bombing. The treasures survived the fighting, and in 1993-94 the pavilions were reconstructed and the stelae reset, a project partially funded by the American Express Foundation.

Beyond the rows of stelae lies the Courtyard of the Sages, a stone-paved plaza leading to the heart of the temple, the Great House of Ceremonies. I followed the wavering, hypnotic sounds of Vietnamese music across the courtyard to the open-air chamber, where I sat down to listen to one of the temple's regular performances of folk music. The half-dozen musicians played traditional instruments—an airy bamboo flute, the expressive *dan bau* with its single string, a 16-stringed zither, or *dan tranh*. An unusual instrument from the Central Highlands, a *k'longput,* was made of large tubes of bamboo lashed together to resemble a pan pipe; it was played by clapping the hands over the open ends of the tubes. At one point, an elfin young woman in a bright red ao dai gave a virtuoso exhibition on a vertical xylophone made of sections of bamboo.

Before I left, I read one of the poems in the guidebook I'd purchased at the temple's bookstore. The words were those of a revered scholar named Nguyen Trai: "Loitering in the evening I contemplate the world, the instant of a bird's flight…. A thousand autumns gone, and water keeps its face. A thousand generations gazing at the moon, yet still herself. Everything is known. Only the human heart remains unfathomed."

At about the time those haunting lines were written, in the 15th century, legend holds that Emperor Le Loi was given a magic sword by a golden tortoise while boating on Hoan Kiem Lake, a few blocks east of the Temple of Literature. The emperor reportedly used the sword to drive the Chinese from Vietnam, afterward returning it to its guardian—a deed that gave Hoan Kiem its name, the Lake of the Restored Sword.

Even in the 15th century, one of the favored gathering spots of Hanoi was along the shore of this small, serene body of water. People still congregate

around Hoan Kiem Lake. Of an early morning they come to jog or to practice t'ai chi. In the afternoon young men gather to play *da cau*—kick badminton—surrounded by crowds of onlookers. Night brings out friends and lovers, who stroll the sidewalks around the shoreline as the city's lights fragment into a million colored shards on the rippled surface of the lake.

"If you go to Hoan Kiem Lake in the afternoon, there are many old men playing chess," Giang said to me. "Very peaceful."

On the northeast side of the lake I visited Ngoc Son Temple, crossing an arching red wooden footbridge to the small island where the temple sits in a bower of trees. I stepped inside the dark, cool shrine, with its altar dedicated to Tran Hung Dao and other Tran dynasty figures. In a museum case just outside were the preserved remains of a giant freshwater tortoise taken from the lake in 1968. The lacquered carcass was the size of a boulder, nearly seven feet long and 550 pounds in weight. So there really were tortoises here. I'd thought the legend of the Restored Sword centered on some mythical creature, but at least the tortoise part of the tale had some relation to fact. Out in the middle of the lake was a small island where the tortoises have laid their eggs for centuries. A pagoda called the Tortoise Tower rises from the islet, a symbol of Hanoi often reproduced in souvenir paintings.

I came back to Hoan Kiem Lake that evening, walking over from my hotel. Near Ngoc Son Temple I passed street photographers with displays of pictures showing couples and families posing by the footbridge. I took a seat on one of the benches that ring the lake, beneath a canopy of fragrant blossoms drooping over the water. Lovers squeezed together on nearby benches. The night was warm, a gentle breeze blowing across the lake. Off to my right were the lights of the Old Quarter. Closer at hand, the bridge to Ngoc Son Temple scribed a black silhouette against the light-flecked water.

In the street that ran around the lake, motorbikes

were circling, their horns beeping constantly. People passed slowly down the sidewalk behind me—two soldiers deep in conversation; a husband and wife, each holding a hand of one of their two children. A young woman hailed a boy on a bike, who pulled over to the curb. The pair stood close, laughing and exchanging pleasantries.

I was struck by the upbeat mood of these people. This was no somnolent Communist capital but a lively, almost festive place. The Vietnamese, who had relatively few material possessions, knew how to find joy in small things, in the chance meeting of a friend on the street, in the beauty of sitting quietly beside a wooden footbridge arching across dark water.

For old times' sake, I decided to take a ride in a pedicab. I recalled the soothing sensation of rocking down the street in one of these three-wheeled contraptions, its fat bicycle tires whirring on the pavement. You didn't get anywhere very fast in a pedicab, but you arrived relaxed, and you had time to see things. I found an empty one a block from the lake, and we set off down the darkened side streets. The air blew warm across my face, thick with the memory-provoking scents of frying food, garbage, and Honda fumes. Along the sidewalks on either side of me, a documentary movie was unfolding, offering glimpses of dozens of lives: In minuscule open-air restaurants, people huddled against walls under naked light bulbs, their shadows harsh and mysterious as they dug into their late night suppers; along the curb, children stopped playing their games to gawk as I rolled by; in darkened alcoves, lit cigarettes glowed like incandescent rubies.

From the quiet back streets we emerged into the carnival-like atmosphere of the Old Quarter, with its gaggle of vendors and promenaders. The stores here have been in the business of supplying every conceivable commodity since the 1400s. The so-called 36 Streets of the Old Quarter are still named for the goods traditionally sold along them: Paper Street, Rice Street, even Vermicelli Street.

I began to wonder if we'd stumbled into T-Shirt

Answering a call to patriotism, Vietnamese of all ages file toward the final resting place of Ho Chi Minh, father of modern-day Vietnam. Ho's remains, like those of Lenin in Moscow and Mao in Beijing, are preserved inside an imposing mausoleum, on Ba Dinh Square. It was from this square that Ho read his nation's Declaration of Independence on September 2, 1945. A decorated war veteran (above) who fought against the French and the Americans attends a military parade in Hanoi.

Street. From shop after shop, racks of cotton goods jutted onto the sidewalk. There were any number of renditions of a grinning Mickey Mouse, and in one shop, a shirt bore the likeness of an angry King Kong, with the single word, "Tyson," emblazoned beneath it. Tintin, the venerable French storybook character, was popular. Cartoon books featuring this spike-haired boy reporter had rolled off Paris presses even as the Viet Minh and the French were slaughtering

one another; it seemed a genuine curiosity that such a peculiarly French creation could permeate Vietnam's culture so deeply that half a century later this Gallic icon would still be popping up on Vietnamese clothing (a phenomenon on the order of the lingering influence of French headgear—illustrated by rheumy-eyed old Vietnamese gents sporting berets).

Whole families were sitting on the sidewalks in front of their shops, a surprising number of which overflowed with stereos and TVs, refrigerators and electric fans. Panasonic, Gold Star, Toshiba, Hitachi—those were the watchwords here. That abundance of goods represented one of the biggest challenges that Vietnam now faces—how to reconcile the growing gulf between haves and have-nots. The Jekyll-and-

Wreckage of a U.S. B-52 bomber, shot down on December 27, 1972, still lies in a northern Hanoi neighborhood. Memories linger of the punishing 11-day "Christmas bombing" of the North, which brought Vietnamese negotiators back to the Paris peace talks and resulted in an agreement to withdraw all U.S. combat troops from Vietnam. To whip up patriotic fervor, captured U.S. pilots were paraded through Hanoi in May 1966.

At Hoa Lo Prison, known as the Hanoi Hilton to American prisoners of war and the Maison Centrale to Vietnamese revolutionaries who were imprisoned there, a guard watches as the notorious landmark is razed to make way for a high-rise hotel and office tower.

Hyde government policy that's evolved over the past decade—the creation of a market economy within a politically totalitarian state—raises knotty questions: How far can the Communist leaders go in allowing economic freedom without permitting a measure of political freedom as well? What lies ahead when the younger generation wants it all?

Pedestrians had to thread their way among the merchandise spilling from the stores. I could easily have touched those people as we inched along the curb, through the taxis and motorbikes that hemmed us in fore and aft. There was a psychedelic effect in being a part of this chaotic throng. People loomed out of the crowd at my elbow like faces in a dream, disappearing just as quickly; passengers on the backseats of motorbikes that wove by beside

my pedicab had a few moments to size me up before they passed on.

Being a lone foreigner amidst that tidal wave of humanity, surrounded by the babble of a strange tongue, I might have had reason for feeling uneasy, yet I detected no unfriendly looks, and there were plenty of smiles directed my way. One dark-eyed little girl with a pageboy haircut ran up to me and shouted, "Hello, welcome." I'd never wished more sincerely that I could speak Vietnamese than at that moment.

A Tribute to Uncle Ho

The early morning sun slanted through the ranks of government buildings that cluster just west of the Old Quarter. Our Toyota rolled down the wide boulevards, past embassy after embassy. Draped across the streets were red banners with gold writing, a welcome to visiting foreign dignitaries. We also passed several placards warning about AIDS, plastered to walls and light posts; the first case of HIV infection was detected here in 1990.

Tung parked just south of Ba Dinh Square. It was here on September 2, 1945, that Ho Chi Minh read his country's Declaration of Independence from France, quoting Thomas Jefferson and the Declaration of the Rights of Man from the French Revolution. I'd seen a grainy black-and-white photograph of that historic moment. The photograph showed the square and all the adjoining streets packed with people. Ho and his entourage stood on a platform surrounded by flags of the new Democratic Republic of Vietnam. That tumultuous scene, in which tens of thousands of Vietnamese expectantly hung on the words of one frail speaker with a wispy goatee, speaks volumes about the veneration accorded Ho Chi Minh. To the Vietnamese, Ho was Thomas Jefferson and George Washington rolled into one. Even today, every denomination of Vietnamese currency bears the portrait of Bac Ho—Uncle Ho.

On Ho's death in 1969, his body was embalmed, and in 1975 it was interred in a mausoleum modeled on Lenin's Tomb and built with Soviet aid. (The whole idea was against Ho's wishes: In his will, he directed that he be cremated.) Giang and I set off down Hung Vuong Street, the thoroughfare that leads past Ba Dinh Square and Ho's final resting place—a squat, severe cubicle surrounded by columns and with an overhanging roof said to represent a lotus flower (I couldn't see it). The Vietnamese had lavished all the pomp they could muster on that gray and red marble structure; it wasn't really handsome, but it was suitably imposing. Off to our right, across an expanse of grass, the National Assembly Building symbolically faced the burial place of the country's fallen leader.

A banner stretched across the front of the tomb. Giang translated its words at my request: "The Vietnamese Communist Party will live forever."

Maybe, but it wouldn't be the unadulterated Communism of Lenin, or even the nationalist-tempered doctrine of Ho Chi Minh. I was recalling the burgeoning consumerism down in the shops of the Old Quarter; the seeds of capitalist prosperity had been planted in the barren Communist soil, and it would be difficult now to restrain their growth. Of course, the unshackling of Vietnam's economy raised an issue that went beyond government designs to perpetuate Communism. You had to wonder what age-old cultural elements would be lost to modernization. In this country where veneration of the past is so strong, it isn't difficult to find Vietnamese who fear the perversion of their culture through the invasion of Western materialism; there is, on the other hand, that element in every emerging nation that regards a McDonald's franchise as the epitome of societal advancement. Will the Golden Arches someday frame the Temple of Literature?

A line stretched from the entrance to Ho's tomb down Hung Vuong Street. Giang and I queued up behind a busload of Taiwanese tourists. The line moved extraordinarily fast. Soon we were facing the entrance, which was flanked by large floral wreaths. Soldiers, as stark as wraiths in their white uniforms, stood on either side of the doorway, rifles at their sides. Other soldiers were positioned out front, directing the visitors to straighten up the line and move along. This was serious business: no cameras, no bags, no hands in the pockets, no talking, no disrespectful demeanors—and keep moving. I felt like Dorothy being ushered in for an audience with the Wizard of Oz.

Then we were inside, where a sudden blast of cold air hit my face. The mausoleum was one big refrigerator. We were herded through so quickly that I don't recall much about the inside of the tomb, except that it was dimly lit and cold. We wound

Monument honoring North Vietnamese antiaircraft gunners marks a spot beside Hanoi's Truc Bach Lake, where U.S. Navy pilot John McCain, today's Arizona senator and one of the conflict's most famous prisoners of war, was captured in 1967 after ejecting from his crippled jet.

down corridors for a ways before reaching the interior chamber. At one point a guard shoved me on the arm (I thought I was moving pretty briskly), and several times the soldiers shushed people who were whispering.

The line formed a U-shape around Ho's glass sarcophagus: down one side of the chamber, across the front by Ho's feet, then up the other side toward the exit. Each of the Taiwanese tourists ahead of me paused briefly at the foot of Ho's casket, turned to face the corpse, and bowed in veneration. I had no idea of how much respect Ho engendered in other Asian nationalities.

That display also set off alarms. Was I expected to bow in respect as well? A sudden image flashed through my mind—of soldiers yanking me out of line and dragging me away for disrespectfulness. As my turn neared to stand before Ho's feet, I debated what to do. Would bowing to the body of Ho Chi Minh be a sign of disrespect to my own countrymen who'd died in Vietnam?

I didn't have much time to ponder the dilemma. Next thing I knew I was standing before Bac Ho. He was a tiny man. His face was alabaster, the skin unnaturally shiny and opaque. He might have been carved from a block of Ivory Soap. In that instant I decided that, former enemy or not, Ho Chi Minh was a giant of this century, and as such deserved the respect given to any leader of that magnitude. I managed an awkward nod and shuffled on. In a matter of seconds I was back outside in the welcome light and warmth.

I followed the crowd a short distance to the Presidential Palace, a grand French provincial mansion built in 1906 to house the governor-generals of Indochina. Today the palace accommodates state guests. After Ho Chi Minh's forces triumphed over the French in 1954, this palace could have been Ho's home, but he refused to live in it, choosing instead to dwell in a lowly two-room stilt-house on the grounds close by. Ho is said to have lived and worked there until he died. Despite its humble quality, the structure

Stretching to greet the day, a Hanoi man begins his exercises at Hoan Kiem Lake, a quiet oasis in the center of town. In the early mornings, many of the capital's residents gravitate to the lake, often to jog or practice t'ai chi.

is quite lovely, all polished wood inside and out, hidden within a garden aflame with bougainvillea.

The house is built in the simple *nha san* style of the Central Highlands: the second-floor living quarters raised above the height of a man by wooden stanchions; a balcony on all sides, with split bamboo shades that can be rolled down to block sun or rain; an open interior to allow cross ventilation. Ho's work desk and bookshelves were in one room (a prominent volume bore Lenin's picture on the dust jacket); the other chamber was a spartan bedroom with a small table and low single bed covered by a rush mat. The Taiwanese tourists and I shuffled along the balcony for a peek inside these quarters. Everything is said to have been left just as it was when Ho was living. The accoutrements were few—an old manual typewriter, an alarm clock, a small radio—but they gleamed like museum pieces.

The house is surrounded by tall palms and the collection of fruit trees that Ho used to tend. Not far away are the hutches in which the Vietnamese leader kept pigeons for a hobby. In the sheltered area beneath the raised home sat a long conference table. It was around this table that Ho met with his commanders during the war against the Americans. Just a few feet away I paused by the edge of a placid pond and watched a swirl of goldfish dimple its surface. Ho used to feed those fish every morning. I could visualize him standing there in that quiet garden, white-haired and wizened, chain-smoking 555-brand cigarettes, choosing to live modestly when he could have had whatever he wished. There was irony in the image of that fragile old man waging war against the mightiest nation on earth from this place of Zen-like repose.

As visitors leave the grounds of the Presidential Palace, they have to run a gauntlet of souvenir shops and food stands, a circumstance at virtually every tourist site in the country. I walked past the rear of the Ho Chi Minh Mausoleum and down the opposite side of Ba Dinh Square from which I'd approached the tomb. Near the far end of the square I came to the

Pedicab driver pauses before Hanoi's Municipal Theatre, built in 1911 as a replica of the Paris Opera House. Although this Hanoi landmark is being restored, high-rise developers have demolished other French colonial-era buildings. City planners maintain they want to modernize Hanoi without sacrificing its low-key character and low-rise charm.

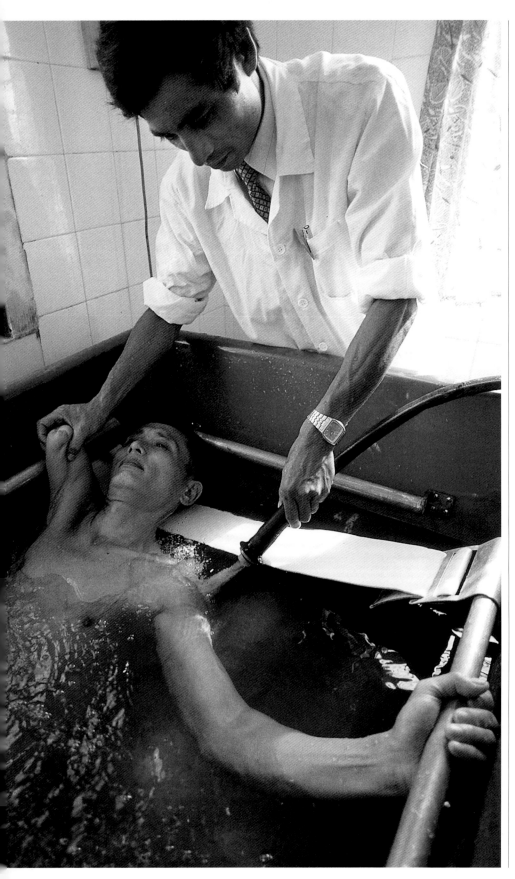

petite One Pillar Pagoda, a quaint testament to gratitude and vindictiveness.

The room-size wooden shrine, which sits on a pedestal in the middle of a lotus pond, was built by the Emperor Ly Thai Tong in 1049. Before his marriage, the heirless emperor had dreamed that he'd met the goddess of mercy, Quan Am; seated on a lotus flower, the goddess had handed him a male child. Shortly afterward the emperor wed a peasant girl, who gave him a male successor. Ly Thai Tong erected this pagoda in thanks, designing it to resemble a lotus flower, the symbol of purity, rising from a sea of sorrow. The pagoda had stood in Hanoi for 900 years, until, in 1954, the vanquished French destroyed it as they evacuated the city, one of the last acts of their *mission civilisatrice*. The new government immediately rebuilt the ancient shrine.

Half a block west of the One Pillar Pagoda stands the Ho Chi Minh Museum, a stark white building in the shape of a lotus flower (its angular, upswept profile actually does resemble a blossom). Inaugurated in May 1990, on the centenary of Ho's birth, the museum houses a bizarre collection of art and artifacts said to illustrate Ho's life and ideals. One startling exhibit, entitled "Guernica 1937," reproduced elements from Picasso's famous painting protesting the Fascist bombing of the Spanish town. Another display, protesting pollution, featured a huge white breakfast table bearing Brobdingnagian pieces of fruit—two apples, a banana, a pineapple, a lemon—set against a mural of smoking factories. Strangest of all was the display on America's failed military effort in Vietnam, symbolized by a 1958 Edsel emerging from a wall. Whoever came up with these juxtapositions should certainly be hailed as a creative thinker.

Creativity was in evidence again that evening when I visited the Thang Long Water Puppet Theatre, Vietnam's finest forum for this ancient art. The neon lights of the theater beckoned along Hoan Kiem Lake. The woman at the front door who punched my ticket offered me a program and a

folding paper fan. I thought that the fan was just a souvenir until I stepped into the second-floor performance hall. In the sultry, steeply inclined gallery, dozens of white fans fluttered like the wings of giant moths.

I found my seat, about four rows up from the edge of the water tank that serves as the stage for the puppets. At the rear of the tank was an elaborate set simulating a red-roofed communal house. A green bamboo curtain hung from the front of the pagoda-like structure. The puppeteers were hidden behind this curtain, standing waist-deep in the tank; they operated their puppets with long poles, which were submerged so that the wooden figures seemed to stand right on the water. This gentle form of entertainment may have come about when puppeteers

were forced to carry on in the face of flooding in the Red River Delta.

In a box above the stage sat a troupe of singers and musicians—both men and women wearing ao dai and dark mandarin-style hats. The 50-minute performance began as their music exploded through the darkened hall. There were 17 acts, each an intricately choreographed story. In the Dragon Dance, four gold dragons thrashed around the stage, two spouting long plumes of water and two with fountaining Roman candles in their mouths. Then came a succession of dancing fairies, leaping fish, wriggling snakes, pouncing foxes, and frolicking phoenixes. Toward the end of the performance, the Emperor Le Loi received his enchanted sword from the golden tortoise in Hoan Kiem Lake.

Healing takes many forms in Hanoi. A university professor who lost an arm in a battle with U.S. cavalrymen undergoes physical therapy at a home for disabled war veterans. Acupuncture eases the pain of others at the Dien Huu Pagoda.

Elderly woman and her granddaughter enter the Quan Thanh Pagoda in Hanoi during the Tet lunar new year festival. Some Vietnamese say satellite television, the Internet, and hundreds of thousands of foreign visitors have widened the generation gap in a culture that puts a premium on parental authority and family ties.

Tempered by the hardships of war and poverty, most Hanoi residents live in austere narrow houses with Buddhist altars that honor family ancestors. As affluence comes to Hanoi, city fathers hope to avoid the congestion, pollution, and squatter colonies that overwhelm other Asian capitals.

A PASTIME FOR THE POLITBURO

Golf? In Vietnam? That's what I thought when I heard about King's Island Golf Resort and Country Club, a Thai-financed development 28 miles west of Hanoi in Ha Tay Province. I arranged to meet the project's construction manager at his Hanoi office. Peter Jensen turned out to be a pleasant young Canadian who was carrying the burden of making this enormous project come to be. Peter laid out a map of the 22-million-dollar resort, which, when completed, would comprise two 18-hole golf courses (one public, one private), a hundred-room hotel, 50 guest villas, and recreational facilities such as equestrian and fitness centers, all on 885 acres of rolling land on the shore of the Dong Mo Reservoir.

"We've got six holes open on one course," Peter

told me. "We held the first tournament in Vietnam two weeks ago, sponsored by the American Chamber of Commerce." When I asked how they'd managed a tournament with only six holes available for play, Peter smiled. "They played three rounds."

Peter introduced me to a friend of his from Vancouver, a businessman named Ross who was in Vietnam looking for potential investments. Ross confided that he marveled at the ambitiousness of Peter's company: "I think it's too soon to sink that kind of money into this country. There's still too much red tape, too much corruption."

Vietnam's cumbersome bureaucracy hasn't stopped foreign investment, though the initial enthusiasm may be subsiding. The fact that big money is flowing into the country is illustrated by the fees that King's Island commands: $15,000 U.S. for an individual membership. Peter said that 300 people had already plunked down that hefty fee, 20 percent of them Vietnamese, the rest mainly Koreans and Japanese. The previous Sunday they'd had 80 golfers on the course.

"Prime Minister Vo Van Kiet was out at our place recently to try his hand at the game," Peter told me. Apparently the prime minister stamped the imperialist pastime as a worthy socialist endeavor. "He had a pretty good swing," said Peter, relating that the prime minister's bodyguards made up a sizable gallery.

Members of the politburo with mashies in their hands—what better proof that a new Vietnam is emerging?

Peter told me that the government is launching its own development adjacent to King's Island, with a complex of villas to be used as a government retreat and a cultural village that will re-create the dwellings of some of Vietnam's 54 ethnic minorities.

One of Peter's challenges in building his golf course has been finding skilled workmen. Naturally, few people knew what the hell a golf course was when he arrived. He was able to hire an army engineering company to do the excavation work. "You should see them out there with those old monster Russian earthmovers of theirs," Peter chuckled. "But they get the job done." The government has opted to keep the army occupied in this new period of peace by allowing military units to operate as private businesses. The alternative is to unleash one of the world's largest standing armies—600,000 men—into an economy already overburdened by 25 percent unemployment. "They might end up with a lot of bandits if they did that," Peter observed.

Peter, Ross, and I boarded the resort's shuttle bus and headed out of the city to visit the development, about an hour and fifteen minutes away. At King's Island we had to take a boat across the reservoir to the clubhouse. The setting was impeccable for the Robert McFarland-designed golf course: a gently

sloping terrain with water a presence on nearly every hole and the verdant Ba Vi Mountains a picture-postcard backdrop. Peter showed me one of the villas that was under construction, a tropical design with tile floors, high ceilings, and sweeping views of the water and mountains.

After lunch at the clubhouse ("the best hamburgers in Vietnam," Peter boasted—the ground beef is flown in from the U.S.) I played a few holes with Peter and Ross. It was tempting to joke about the ready availability of bunkers in Vietnam, but when I considered that King's Island was able to supply dozens of Vietnamese with good-paying jobs, I realized what a tremendous boon to the area this improbable-sounding enterprise really was.

By now it was getting close to my scheduled time to leave Hanoi. Before I departed the capital, I returned to Hoan Kiem Lake in the evening, settling onto a lakeside bench. Recollections began welling up of the many individuals whose lives had touched mine over the past few days—the ragged child beggars outside the Nha Noi Ho Tay floating restaurant at West Lake, chanting their mantras of "no mama, no papa" while they tugged on my arm...those white-clad soldiers guarding Ho Chi Minh's tomb, going about their jobs with grim determination... that little girl in the Old Quarter who'd so cheerily welcomed me to her world...my young caddy at King's Island, Hien, smiling shyly as she handed me my club.

I thought of all the Vietnamese—and of the millions of Americans—whose lives had been altered by the war. In particular I thought about the people on both sides who still cannot let go of their anger, who will never be able to forgive and move on. It is those aggrieved souls who remain prisoners of war.

Personally, I felt liberated to have visited Hanoi. Old stereotypes and preconceptions were loosening their grip, and new avenues of experience had swung into view. I was eager now to set off on more of those unexplored roads.

Lotus blossoms, symbol of purity in Vietnamese mythology, cover lakes and ponds across the capital. Vietnamese buildings, including Ho Chi Minh's tomb, sometimes have architectural details that echo the lotus flower's distinctive shape.

Leisurely summer sun hangs on the horizon as boaters watch night fall on West Lake. Largest of the many lakes that dapple Hanoi, West Lake lies in an ancient bed of the Red River.

Chapter 2

Northern Encounters: Halong Bay and Beyond

To Americans who came of age in the sixties—legally, politically, or otherwise—countless Vietnamese place-names are still loaded with indelible memories...names such as the Gulf of Tonkin. In that body of water lapping northern Vietnam and the southernmost China coast, an incident occurred in the summer of 1964 that would mark a turning point in our nation's history. (I'd just finished high school at the time and was idling pleasantly toward college.) That August, American naval forces came under attack while patrolling off North Vietnam, prompting the U.S. Congress to pass the Tonkin Gulf Resolution—Lyndon Johnson's carte blanche authorization to wage war against the North Vietnamese.

I intended to visit one portion of the Gulf of Tonkin—less for its wartime associations than for its remarkable beauty. The thousand-square-mile section of the gulf called Halong Bay has long been regarded as one of the natural wonders of Southeast Asia. In 1994, UNESCO deemed it worthy of designation as a World Heritage Site. Dotted with some 3,000 fancifully eroded limestone isles, the bay is often compared to Guilin, China—that magical landscape of craggy karst formations depicted in thousands of silk paintings, wreathed in clouds and wisps of greenery.

The islands of Halong Bay are riddled with caves and are often swathed in fog. They poke up mysteriously from the blue-green waters of the gulf like a miniature range of misty mountains. About half of Cat Ba, one of the larger islands—known for its fine forests, lakes, and beaches—is protected by a national park. The bay was featured in several scenes of the

In a familiar countryside scene, farm boys play with an obedient water buffalo along National Highway 1 in the former Demilitarized Zone (DMZ) that once separated North and South Vietnam. The heavily bombed 6.2-mile-wide buffer zone is now awash in rice, Vietnam's chief export crop.

movie *Indochine*—the sequence in which the rene-
gade French officer and his Vietnamese lover drift
aboard their junk, lost among nameless isles.

To reach Halong Bay, a hundred miles east of
Hanoi, meant a long, hard drive over stretches of
abominable road. The good news was that the route
led through a landscape of incomparable beauty, the
green-on-green rice bowl of the Red River Delta. I
loaded my gear on a gray morning when low tatters

of clouds were shaking out intermittent showers. As
usual, the road was jammed with traffic. The seemingly endless ragtag periphery of Hanoi was home to
small factories, warehouses, garages, and shops. What
an amazing collection of goods sat in front of those
places: piles of logs and heaps of tires, mounds of
plastic pipe and stacks of bricks, motorbike cowlings
and electric motors, handcrafted benches and gaudy
wardrobes.

It took a good while to escape the city, but finally we were rolling past miles of paddies, mist-robed
mountains in the distance. Because rice is grown in
more than one season here, with different stages of
the growing cycle occurring simultaneously, the
paddies formed a checkerboard of emerald, olive,
chartreuse. This was the Vietnam that sticks in

*Rendezvous in the Tonkin Gulf: A Navy
F-4 Phantom loaded with Sidewinder
and Sparrow air-to-air missiles appears
over an aircraft carrier on Yankee
Station, the Seventh Fleet's staging area.*

*Mammoth cruise liner dwarfs a tiny
sampan in the fog-shrouded waters of
Halong Bay, where some 3,000 rocky
islands rise from the Tonkin Gulf. Cruise
ships now bring thousands of tourists,
including former American GIs, to
Vietnam each year.*

*Following pages: Sampans ply the placid
waters of Halong Bay. In Vietnamese,
the name Halong Bay means Where the
Dragon Descends into the Sea.*

Young women ride in the rain through the Haiphong central market, where a public letter writer still caters to the illiterate. One of Vietnam's most important seaports, Haiphong came under ferocious American air and naval attacks between 1965 and 1968, and again in 1972, when President Richard Nixon ordered the mining of Haiphong harbor to stop the flow of Soviet supplies.

the mind—the timeless, unbelievably lush countryside, with its atmosphere of calm detachment from the hurried complications of the rest of the world. My best-preserved image of rural Vietnam came to me while flying back to Saigon from a field assignment late one afternoon during the war. As the C-130 I was aboard banked over the swampy terrain surrounding the southern capital, the setting sun flared off paddies that seemed to go on forever, turning the flooded fields to burnished copper.

Surprisingly, that vista of endless paddies was misleading. Only about 20 percent of Vietnam's mountainous landscape is arable, with most of the rice-growing land concentrated in the Red River and Mekong Deltas—the reason the country's physical profile is often likened to two rice baskets suspended

at opposite ends of a long pole. Farmers in the Red River Delta harvest two crops each year, while in the warmer south, the Mekong Delta yields three crops.

The sharp increase in Vietnam's rice production over the past few years is graphic proof of the success of the country's new market-driven economy. In the late 1970s, collectivization and natural disasters had reduced the rice crop so severely that some people were foraging for roots to keep from starving. (The Vietnamese eat three-quarters of a pound of rice per person each day; in the U.S., the average per person consumption is 22 pounds a *year.*) The lack of food was at least partly to blame for the mass exodus of boat people from Vietnam in 1979. The situation started to improve shortly after the government began implementing its economic reforms in 1986, in which central planning was reduced and the development of private enterprise permitted.

Under the new policy, called *doi moi*—economic restructuring—land that had been confiscated in the south was returned to its rightful owners, and family farming began to be encouraged instead of state-run farms. The result: Since the mid-1980s, when Vietnam had to import rice to feed its people, the country has become the world's third largest rice exporter, producing over 20 million tons a year and exporting about three million tons. Rice, crude oil, and coal now account for the lion's share of the country's export earnings. To protect those earnings—and to safeguard against future food shortages—Vietnam has banned the conversion of rice fields for industrial use.

Incomes for farmers have jumped along with the higher levels of rice production, rising some 200 percent since 1990. Of course, that's starting from near the bottom of the economic scale. The contrasts between today's generally better-off city folk and the perennially impoverished farmers— about 70 percent of Vietnam's population—are often as sharp as the gulf between mandarins and peasants of long ago. That's one reason for the steady migration of country people to the cities, a trend that may be accelerating, with potentially disastrous results. Too many of those unskilled farmers end up as unemployed residents of urban shantytowns.

Along the highway toward Halong Bay were rural scenes little changed in centuries—the slow-paced ritual of farmers stooping to plant their flooded fields, children astride plodding water buffaloes, women in conical hats endlessly dipping buckets in ditches of muddy water. Prowling egrets stood out ghostly white against the green fields, moving like stiff, tentative stilt walkers on their long yellow legs. Now and then I spotted scarecrows of crossed sticks standing watch over plots of rice seedlings; their tattered shirts and old straw hats would have looked at home in an Iowa cornfield. On the crowded road, we passed two-wheeled carts pulled by stolid zebu oxen, and rickety buses filled to overflowing, the passengers'

belongings lashed to the rooftops. Now and then we drove over brown carpets of rice, spread across the highway to dry before milling.

Our route led through numerous small towns, which hugged the road in dusty disarray, the rice fields edging right up to the backs of the houses. Scrawny, fearless dogs slept along the roadway, oblivious to the whir of traffic. What went on in those isolated villages? Probably much the same thing that had gone on 500 years before, only now some of the houses sported television antennas.

Occasionally we passed a walled area rising from the fields—the local cemetery. A few large compounds sat out in the middle of nowhere, military bases, according to Giang. These were usually in the best repair of any of the buildings we saw, some-

times freshly whitewashed, with bold red banners unfurled across the front.

Once we passed a long line of people repairing a dike. They were stretched from the brink of the water into the adjacent paddy, passing cinder-block-size chunks of wet black earth down the line in bucket-brigade fashion. That age-old ritual seemed comparable to Egyptian peasants toiling to build the pyramids, or serfs laboring on the Great Wall of China.

Just as antique in appearance were the road-repair crews we happened upon. Like most of the highways in Vietnam I would travel, the stretch of road between Hanoi and Halong Bay was a nightmare in places, a pocked and rutted strip that tossed me around inside the back of the Toyota like a bug in a jar. Along some of the worst sections of highway, we

Low clouds hang over the rugged Hoang Lien Mountains, sometimes called the Tonkinese Alps, as a mother and child of the Hmong ethnic minority walk a winding road near the old French hill station of Sa Pa, northwest of Hanoi.

U.S. Air Force F-111 bomber races low over the lonely triple-canopy jungle of North Vietnam. Early versions of the warplane's sophisticated terrain-hugging radar caused a series of fatal crashes, and the Pentagon finally withdrew the F-111 from Southeast Asia combat.

Young Hmong woman carries goods in a handmade basket, while the hands of a village elder betray decades of back-breaking toil in the isolated mountains near the China border. The Hmong, who number some 750,000 and live throughout the highlands of Vietnam's nine northernmost provinces, have no written language, passing on their literature and folklore by word of mouth.

Pages 60-61: Northern hill tribes cultivate rice in irrigated terraces etched into craggy hills above Lao Cai in northwest Vietnam. Many ethnic minorities continue to slash and burn whole hillsides to grow maize, their dietary mainstay. Teaching the Hmong and others to practice sedentary agriculture has long been a government goal.

encountered bands of women toting rocks in large, shallow pans. Into the holes went their armloads of rocks. By the side of the highway there would be a drum of asphalt simmering over a fire, giving off billowing clouds of black smoke. Workers dipped metal containers tied to the ends of poles into the hot tar, which they then slopped over the rocks.

It was a shock to see all those 90-pound women staggering around with their heavy loads. That seemed like a job for men. Most of the workers in the fields were also women. In truth, Vietnamese women have traditionally done most of the physical labor (according to a government study, women annually put in 2.07 times as many hours as men). While Vietnamese men engage in trades such as fishing or carpentry, when it comes to jobs requiring nothing more than

a strong back, women often get the call. In one agricultural cooperative that was studied, nearly half of the women suffered from backbone diseases as a result of carrying heavy loads.

As the Toyota bounced along, we were constantly overtaking one lumbering vehicle after another. It was apparent that in Vietnam there is no such thing as a passing zone. Hills, blind curves, any place will do. If everyone tries to pass at once, so much the better. These maneuvers are made more challenging by the fact that vehicles being overtaken often move closer to the center of the highway in order to block the view of the drivers behind them. And I swear that truck drivers would put on a burst of speed whenever we started to go around. It must have been a point of honor for them not to be passed.

Tung routinely swerved into the other lane into a stream of oncoming traffic. What looked to be certain head-on collisions were avoided at the last moment as the vehicles bearing down on us veered toward the shoulder just far enough to allow our Toyota to pass with inches to spare. This automotive ballet of terror was played out to the background music of grinding gears, laboring engines, and squalling horns. Small wonder that highway crashes are common in Vietnam. All along the roads I saw little white plaster Buddhist shrines that had been erected wherever someone had died.

WHERE THE DRAGON DESCENDS INTO THE SEA

Looking across immense, island-stippled Halong Bay, I saw at once why so much praise has been lavished on this region. It *was* a setting like those in a Chinese painting: Red-sailed junks glided slowly among legions of rough-hewn isles, which emerged from a waveless sea tinted pewter by an overcast sky.

Around noon we reached the town of Bai Chay, the hub of area sight-seeing activities. After lunch (fried fish only minutes out of the bay), we set out to explore those myriad isles aboard one of the tourist junks crowding the waterfront. (Helicopter tours are available, but their aerial views don't afford a good look at the many hidden grottoes, and such a noisy, high-tech approach seems at odds with the bay's quiet timelessness.) I bought a map from one of the peddlers working the docks, then we tramped aboard a boat that Giang selected, a weathered vessel of indeterminate color named the *Haiau*—the *Seagull*. It could accommodate about two dozen passengers. Benches were positioned around the deck, with a central seating area roofed over to provide protection against the sun and rain.

The captain and his two deckhands busied themselves with casting off, and we were soon underway, putt-putting away from shore in a cloud of smoke. The crew raised the boat's red canvas sails, though there was hardly enough wind to fill them. They flapped lazily to and fro like stiff red bedsheets

Members of the colorful Dao, foreground, and Hmong hill tribes frequent the market in Sa Pa, where they sell indigo clothing and other handicrafts. Once the alpine retreat of French administrators, Sa Pa was pillaged by Chinese soldiers during a brief border war with Vietnam in 1979. Today hundreds of tourists travel the rugged road to Sa Pa in search of rustic charm and cool mountain temperatures.

on a line. I'd paid for a four-hour cruise, enough time to reach Hang Luon—an island with a secret at its center—and a couple of other interesting islands.

Just outside the harbor we motored past the mainland town of Hon Gai, site of the country's largest anthracite mine. Some 90 percent of Vietnam's coal is mined near here. The presence of coal hereabouts relates to the origin of Halong Bay: The entire region was once part of an ancient seabed that eroded to expose the thousands of limestone islands we see today. Limestone, of course, is composed of compressed organic matter, largely the remains of ancient plants and animals that sank to the seafloor after they died. Coal is also made up of the decomposed remains of aquatic plants and animals, mashed together under tremendous pressure.

Now it happens that 40 percent of the world's petroleum reserves are found in just such sedimentary formations. And *that* is why the world's petroleum companies are scrambling to line up drilling rights for Vietnam's considerable offshore oil deposits, estimated at up to three billion barrels. The deposits were discovered off the coast near Vung Tau before 1975 by American oil companies. In recent years, Vietnam has signed dozens of contracts for oil and gas exploration, with companies from the U.S., Canada, France, the Netherlands, Australia, Japan, and other countries.

Those potential undersea riches have produced friction with Vietnam's neighbor to the north. China has claimed several islands that Vietnam regards as its own—the Paracel Islands, 185 miles east of Danang, and the Spratlys, 295 miles southeast of Nha Trang (located closer to Borneo than Vietnam, the Spratlys have also been claimed by the Philippines, Malaysia, Indonesia, and Taiwan). Sovereignty over those essentially worthless island chains confers territorial rights to oil reserves in a huge swath of the South China Sea.

Geology provides one explanation for the origin of Halong Bay, though admittedly a prosaic one. More interesting is the Vietnamese legend about the

bay's formation. The story holds that a great dragon's thrashing tail dug out a series of valleys here, and as the dragon plunged into the sea the valleys filled with water, leaving the higher land visible as islands. The name Halong Bay means Where the Dragon Descends into the Sea. Local fishermen still report sightings of a giant marine creature known as the Tarasque. If you're willing to pay, you can find someone to take you in search of the monster.

Near Lao Cai, the afterglow of sunset fires the Red River with its namesake hue. Flowing from its source in the Yunnan region of China, the Red River sweeps across the north of Vietnam toward the Gulf of Tonkin. The river's fertile delta is home to some nine-tenths of the population of the north.

I stayed alert for undersea creatures as we motored out into the dragon's lair, but all I saw were rank upon rank of islands, lumps of black or gray rock streaked with rusty browns and blotched with vegetation. This day, the islands receded in a haze under the lowering sky. The drizzle and fog we were encountering typically cloak the bay for several months each year, but the inclement weather only adds to the air of mystery here. Sometimes roiling black clouds hang low, their ragged underbellies nearly touching the rumpled crests of the islands. At such times the land and clouds stretching away into the distance form mirror images of one another, as if the islands have been inverted and pasted in the sky.

Ceaseless waves and gnawing mollusks have eroded the islands into the most fantastic shapes,

Bananas bound for China cross the border at Lao Cai in the remote northwestern corner of Vietnam. Cross-border trade in everything from Vietnamese fruit and vegetables to Chinese beer and fertilizer has accelerated, but memories linger of the 1979 border war that leveled Lao Cai.

Following pages: Small boats glide along the Swallow River toward the Perfume Pagoda, one of Vietnam's most popular tourist destinations, set amid the karst formations of Hoa Binh Province southwest of Hanoi.

Capital of Quang Binh Province, Dong Hoi suffered heavy U.S. bomb damage during the Vietnam War. A skeleton of the city's Roman Catholic church (opposite) is a ghostly reminder that not every bomb hit its target. Farther south, below the former DMZ at Quang Tri, U.S. Marines take a break from fighting near an abandoned Catholic basilica.

with rain and underground streams dissolving their limestone innards to create stalagmite- and stalactite-filled caverns. Watching these endlessly varied stone sculptures drift by was like gazing at clouds. I saw the outlines of castles and cottages, great pyramids and towering icebergs. I wasn't the first to indulge in such flights of fancy here. The names of the islands reflect the work of some active imaginations: Monkey Island, Dragon Island,

Toad Island, Father and Son Rock, the Unicorn.

Sampans carrying families of fishermen ghosted across the glassy sea, playing hide-and-seek among the rock formations. The low wooden boats seemed to have been placed out here in this giant Zen rock garden simply for effect, their red sails a vivid contrast against the dark, scrub-covered isles. With the absence of wind, the sampans and junks drifted dreamlike. Sometimes their owners pulled lethargically on long oars, though the idea of heading anywhere in particular within this vast stony labyrinth seemed purposeless; one place was as good as another. On occasion we passed several boats lying at anchor, rafted together in a floating village. The children of these boat people scrambled from one vessel to the next as nimbly as if they were playing on a grassy field.

After about an hour, we approached Hang Luon, passing through an opening between two shear-sided islands called the Gate to Heaven. Hang Luon itself spread across the water in the shape of a massive stone mushroom, its surface gnarled and pitted. There was a dark opening in the rock along the waterline, wide and downward curving like the open mouth of a giant grouper—Luon Cave, Giang called it. "Do you want to see?" You bet.

The captain of the *Haiau* anchored 50 yards or so off Hang Luon. No sooner had we stopped than a fleet of small boats surrounded us. An ancient fisherwoman with a blue scarf on her head held up a basket of fresh shrimp for my inspection.

"We can go closer in this," said Giang, pointing to one of the craft jostling alongside. The boatman pulled his vessel closer so that Giang and I could climb down. The craft, called a *thuyen nan*, was about the size of a johnboat, maybe 15 feet long. It was constructed of woven strips of bamboo that had been tarred inside and out. Water sloshed around underfoot inside the semiporous boat, but we all sat high and dry on boards laid across the gunwales.

The lean, amiable boatman rowed us into the mouth of the cave, whose ceiling was only a few feet above our heads. Pale-colored stalactites dripped down like huge sharks' teeth. Two young women from another tourist junk were swimming inside the grotto, their bare legs flashing white just below the surface. The shallow water was a luminescent jade, as if lit from below.

We passed on through the cave and emerged *inside* the circular island, in a perfectly round lake several dozen yards across. It was open to the sky, surrounded by high rock walls. We were alone in our little boat on this pool of flat-calm water. It was a mystical place, a spiritual place. The only sounds were the splash of the boatman's oars and the chatter of birds hidden in the patches of greenery. It was as if we'd discovered some drowned volcano where Captain Nemo and the *Nautilus* could have surfaced at any moment.

The boatman gestured toward some graffiti on the rocks above—a few words in Russian, scrawled in irregular white Cyrillic letters. "He says a Russian submarine slipped in here to hide in 1962," Giang interpreted. "The crewmen painted that on the rocks." Shades of Captain Nemo! I suddenly wondered if those reported sightings of the dragon Tarasque might have been based on more than myth, perhaps a sea monster from St. Petersburg.

As we pulled away from the island on the way back to port, a large bird circled overhead. We hadn't encountered much evidence of wildlife out here on the bay, although Giang said one of the islands has a population of yellow-haired monkeys, and that the island called Tuan Chau once had a herd of deer, but the deer were gone. Tuan Chau did boast a small herd of humans. The island had once been a holiday retreat for Ho Chi Minh. It took some readjustment in my conception of Uncle Ho to imagine him taking a vacation.

On one of Ho's trips to Halong Bay, he brought along a Communist buddy. Giang pointed to a smallish hunk of rock we were passing and provided its name—Hon Ti Top. "Ho Chi Minh named that in honor of Marshall Tito." Ho and the longtime

Yugoslav leader had come here together in the 1950s.

Closer to Bai Chay we passed Dau Go Cave—the Cave of Wooden Stakes. It was inside that cavern that the 13th-century defender of Vietnam, Tran Hung Dao, stockpiled the sharpened wooden stakes he used in defeating the Mongol invasion fleet on the Bach Dang River. The sight of the cave drove home the realization of just how deep history lies on this land. Every rock seems to be tied to some ancient

Lobbing grenades at close range, U.S. infantrymen battle North Vietnamese regulars south of the DMZ. Today U.S. bases like Camp Carroll, Con Thien, and the Rockpile have been turned into plantations producing peppers, jackfruit, and rubber. Tens of thousands of North Vietnamese soldiers and truck drivers killed along the nearby Ho Chi Minh Trail are buried in Truong Son National Cemetery in the former DMZ.

battle or glorious deed—a thought that's really not hard to accept when you consider that for the past 2,000 years literally millions of combatants have surged back and forth across this little patch of earth.

By the time we returned to the docks at Bai Chay the sun was settling low. We would be staying the night here and returning to Hanoi in the morning. Bai Chay was mostly a vertical arrangement, clinging to the seaside hills like some Asian Swiss village. Leaving the pavement, Tung drove up a dusty lane leading to the Viet Nhat "minihotel," one of the mom-and-pop operations with a half-dozen rooms that have proliferated in the last few years.

After hauling my gear up to the top floor of the five-story, elevatorless hotel, I set out in search of dinner. Giang had recommended one of the restaurants

Army cavalrymen ride helicopters to help lift the siege at Khe Sanh, where U.S. Marines withstood a 77-day onslaught in early 1968. The battle turned out to be a ruse to tie down American troops while Communist forces attacked South Vietnamese cities during the Tet holiday. Today farmers grow cassava and coffee atop the wind-whipped battlefield.

we'd passed at the bottom of the hill. In the fading light, Bai Chay's feeble nightlife was kicking into gear. The evening's activity appeared to consist almost exclusively of people gathered around the flickering screens of TV sets in the front rooms of houses and hotels. The nasal singing of local television beauties rolled out to greet me as I passed by. Vietnam may be one of the poorest nations on earth—unless you measured wealth in TV sets.

Next morning I sat in my hotel's tiny reception area, sharing a cup of tea with the grandmother of the family that ran the place. The frail old lady perched lightly on a sofa directly across from my chair, never taking her eyes off me. She kept refilling my teacup each time I drank. She didn't speak a word of English, and I'd about exhausted my vocabulary

of smiles and nods, but it was pleasant sitting there with her. When Giang appeared with Tung and began loading my baggage, I said goodbye to the old woman with a bow. She stood in the doorway as we drove away. Painted above the inside of the doorway was a cheery farewell message: "See you again."

On the return to Hanoi, we followed a route that took us farther south than our trip of the day before, passing through Haiphong, the north's largest port. We had to cross two stretches of water aboard ferries, including the broad brown Bach Dang River, where the Vietnamese had sunk the Mongol fleet seven centuries earlier. The wharves of Haiphong were crowded with ships. We'd bombed the hell out of those wharves during the war, losing more than 300 planes to Russian missiles. In 1972, President Nixon ordered the mining of the harbor to choke off Soviet military supplies; the next year, as part of the Paris Peace Accords, the U.S. agreed to help clear the mines.

Today, a smattering of pagodas and colonial architecture offsets the rusty clutter of Haiphong's harbor. Crowds of vacationers now pass through the port city on the way to the beaches and casino of Do Son just to the south. That casino—the country's sole legal gambling den—is off-limits to the Vietnamese; only foreigners are permitted to lose their shirts.

RIDING THE TRANSINDOCHINOIS RAILWAY

Back in the capital, I considered heading up into the pine-clad Hoang Lien Mountains northwest of Hanoi—to the town of Sa Pa. The old French hill station sits in the shadow of the country's highest peak, 10,300-foot Fan Si Pan, whose summit is sometimes dusted with snow. From Sa Pa, you can hike along Vietnam's border with China, or even if you're not up for a mountain trek, you get to see some of the colorfully dressed members of the Hmong and Dao tribes. Each weekend, the Montagnards wend down out of the surrounding mountains to bring their handicrafts to market.

This time, however, I decided to start in the opposite direction, booking overnight passage on the train to Hue—the old imperial capital of Vietnam, a little over 400 miles down the coast south of Hanoi. Around seven in the evening, Tung drove Giang and me to the station, in the heart of the city just west of Hoan Kiem Lake. The light was already failing, and the ancient capital, despite its worn and shabby aspect, looked exotically appealing, the way an aging beauty might appear in the dim light of a smoky bar.

On the train platform, a line of ancient passenger cars awaited us, the pale green carriages of the old Transindochinois railway, a colonial legacy dating from 1899. The French had labored for 37 years to connect Hanoi and Saigon with train service, completing the laying of the narrow-gauge tracks just in time for World War II.

During our 15-hour journey to Hue, the train

would be blazing along at an average speed of a little over 25 miles per hour. If I'd been going on to Saigon, the ride could have lasted up to 52 hours. In the heyday of the Transindochinois, the 1,072-mile Hanoi-Saigon run took as few as 40 hours, but that was when the equipment was newer, and before the tracks had been blown up and repaired untold times in the course of 30 years of warfare.

In the U.S. bombing campaigns against North Vietnam, railways had been prime targets. When all the fighting finally ended in 1975, the Vietnamese faced a massive rebuilding project, and by the time the *Reunification Express* finally began rolling between Hanoi and Saigon, on December 31, 1976, Vietnamese engineers had repaired more than 1,300 bridges, 150 stations, and two dozen tunnels. (The

Holding a rusted .50-caliber machine-gun shell, an impoverished farmer who supplements family income by collecting war booty says the red laterite soil of the Khe Sanh battlefield is both difficult to farm and sometimes deadly: People step on shells or mines plowing the fields or looking for steel. Unexploded shells await scrap-metal buyers from as far away as Hong Kong and Singapore. An American combat boot with a bullet hole bears testimony to the Battle of Khe Sanh's cost—205 U.S. Marines killed and perhaps 15,000 North Vietnamese dead.

Doing what comes naturally, a Vietnamese boy in the provincial capital of Dong Ha peers down the barrel of a derelict U.S. M-48 tank. Dong Ha, situated on National Highway 1 just south of the former DMZ, was a U.S. Marine Corps command center during the Vietnam War.

With no fixed front lines in Vietnam, U.S. commanders depended on mobility to carry the fight deep into uninhabited jungles like the A Shau Valley near the Laotian border. Helicopters ferried artillerymen and their howitzers to hasty hilltop fortifications called firebases to support airborne infantry.

quality of the repairs has often been poor, a fact you can corroborate with the seat of your pants as the lumbering train shimmies and shakes along these ancient tracks.)

Passengers hung out the open windows of the cars, saying their good-byes to friends or stocking up on food, drink, and cigarettes from the ubiquitous peddlers. Giang and I scrambled up the steps of one of the carriages and made our way along the narrow corridor to our compartment. There was much confusion as passengers searched for their seats, struggling by one another with their luggage. The windows on both sides of the car were open, allowing a bit of air to flow through the stuffy coach. Mesh screens covered the lower sections of the aisle windows, evidently to keep children from tumbling out.

At the precise minute of our scheduled departure, the train gave a lurch. We were underway. The Transindochinois! This was travel at its visceral best, our ears assaulted by the grating of the wheels, a hot breeze blowing in through the windows, all of us swaying in our seats. I stepped out into the corridor and braced myself next to the open window. It was black night now. I watched the city slide away, a succession of hovels and shops and new, whitewashed villas. I had been to the capital of Communist Vietnam and had found it much like any other foreign capital—a pastiche of government schemes and private dreams, peopled by the rich and poor and struggling in-betweens.

Here in the corridor, a constant stream of passengers stretched their legs or checked out the doings in other compartments. Giang spent his time smoking cigarettes and flipping the glowing butts out the window into the darkness.

Now and then we would stop for a short while in one of the stations along the way. At each stop vendors hopped on board, passing through the train with trays of candy, gum, cigarettes, drinks. Once, a battalion of vendors pushed carts of steaming *pho* (noodle soup) down the corridor, ladling out the fragrant liquid and sprinkling wads of fresh greens atop each serving. Giang purchased a bowl and slurped it down with noisy gusto.

When it was time for bed, we spread out the thin rush "cushions" that came with each fold-down, board-hard bunk. During the night we passed through several unseen cities with musical names. What transpired, I wondered, in Nam Dinh, Ninh Binh, Thanh Hoa, and Vinh? By all accounts we hadn't missed a lot in terms of scenery; the area around Vinh is said to be one of the poorest in the country, a monotony of bad soil and harsh weather, although just a short distance west of Ninh Binh is the mountain rain forest of Cuc Phuong National Park, a Noah's Ark of wild species that was personally dedicated by Ho Chi Minh in 1963.

Sometime around dawn we passed into Quang Binh Province. As the sun rose higher, the carriage came to life. Giang joined me in the corridor, where he stood brushing his teeth, spitting his rinse-water out the window. Attendants passed down the aisle doling out tasteless sweet rolls. The scenery now was altogether different from the endless flat paddy fields around Hanoi. This was hilly terrain, with patchy fields of rice and corn interspersed with scrubby bushes and small scattered peaks. Meager thatch-roofed huts attested to the region's hardscrabble nature.

After a stop in the city of Dong Hoi, we crossed into Quang Tri Province, formerly the boundary between North and South Vietnam. Here the country had been partitioned in 1954, along the Ben Hai River, with the Demilitarized Zone extending for three miles on both sides of the demarcation line.

Usually no more than a few fragments of bone or teeth, the remains of U.S. soldiers and airmen missing in action are repatriated to American soil in a solemn military ceremony at Hanoi's Noi Bai International Airport. The U.S. honor guard places remains aboard a military transport plane bound for the Army's Central Identification Laboratory in Honolulu, Hawaii.

Just south of the DMZ was where Secretary of Defense Robert McNamara envisioned a barrier built clear across Vietnam to block infiltration, a latter-day Maginot Line.

We stopped once more before Hue, in the town of Dong Ha. The land now flattened out again, huge rice fields stretching into the distance. From Dong Ha, National Highway 9 runs west into the mountains and neighboring Laos. Looking on a map, I saw names dotted along that road that are still capable of stirring the American psyche: Cam Lo, Camp Carroll, the Rockpile, Khe Sanh—the old U.S. military bases that were the nearest thing to a front line in that hit-and-run war. At Khe Sanh, U.S. Marines withstood a two-and-a-half-month siege early in 1968, one of the bloodiest and most publicized battles of the war—and later understood to be part of the diversionary tactics for the larger Tet Offensive, the military defeat that became a psychological victory for the Communists, as they shocked Americans by bringing the war right into the U.S. Embassy compound in Saigon.

These days, coffee and tea plantations stipple the hills around Khe Sanh, and the former DMZ is green with rubber trees and paddies. But it's those abandoned military bases that attract the day-trippers out of Hue. Anyone venturing here should beware, for this is a landscape haunted by the ghosts of dead warriors. Over 200 U.S. Marines and perhaps 15,000 North Vietnamese troops died at Khe Sanh alone.

The old battlegrounds are deadly still: Since 1975, at least 5,000 Vietnamese have been killed or maimed by the unexploded shells and bombs that litter the landscape. The casualties include farmers plowing their fields, as well as scavengers searching for shell casings and other bits of metal to sell to scrap dealers. The scavengers have unearthed a remarkable array of U.S. equipment, including a whole bulldozer, it's claimed. They occasionally turn up old American dog tags and sell them as souvenirs, although thanks to Vietnamese ingenuity, the dog tags peddled to tourists are just as likely to be fake.

CHAPTER 3

Cradles of Culture: Hue and Danang

THE PLATFORM at the Hue train station was vaulted by a dome of the deepest blue sky. In traveling nearly halfway down the coast we'd left behind the perpetually gray days I'd grown used to. But by trading in those overcast skies, we'd also given up the moderate temperatures of the north. It was hot now, though not quite the stifling heat I remembered from my year in Saigon.

Outside the station, Giang led the way toward a well-traveled gold Peugeot station wagon parked in a patch of shade. A slender man in a natty sport shirt and sunglasses stood beside the car—Ngoc, the driver for the next leg of my journey. Ngoc had a neat black mustache and a wry expression, and we found we were able to speak to each other in snippets of English and French.

The ride from the train station to the hotel was a short one, straight up Le Loi Street along the southeast bank of the wide, clear Perfume River. We were in the New City, as this section of Hue is called (at one time it was known as the European Quarter). Across the river, in the old part of Hue, loomed the gray stone walls of the Citadel, the moated fortress-city built by Gia Long, the first emperor of the Nguyen dynasty, Vietnam's last imperial family. Gia Long moved the royal capital to Hue from Hanoi in 1802, after reuniting the country for the first time in two centuries. He and 12 of his descendants ruled from here until 1945, when Emperor Bao Dai abdicated to a delegation dispatched by Ho Chi Minh. (Now in his 80s, Bao Dai is still living out half a century of exile in France.)

Set amid gentle hills some ten miles inland from the coast, Hue has been celebrated for

Timeworn archway lends a window on the Citadel, the walled city in Hue where 13 Nguyen emperors, Vietnam's final dynasty, ruled from 1804 to 1945. During the 1968 Tet Offensive, Communist troops occupied Hue for more than three weeks. U.S. and South Vietnamese forces ousted them in fierce house-to-house fighting that destroyed or damaged large parts of the Citadel.

centuries as Vietnam's center of culture, education, and religion. It's the city of lovers and kings, where history has been both kind and cruel. The very names Hue and the Perfume River conjure up romantic images of warm nights when couples drift in pleasure sampans, of a mighty empire fallen asunder, the tombs of its royalty slumbering in the jungly green countryside below the Imperial Screen Mountain. Hue is the gentle soul of Vietnam, a prosperous, tourist-oriented city of around 250,000 people—much cleaner than other Vietnamese cities, with air that's still breathable.

On the way to my hotel we passed the two bridges that join the new city and the old—Phu Xuan and Trang Tien—temporal links, in effect, between the present and past. Gliding over the first bridge were flocks of dainty teenage schoolgirls; they rode their bicycles with a dignified decorum, sitting ramrod straight and holding the tails of their ao dai to keep them from catching in their spokes—as if their sole purpose in life was to cut the most striking figure possible. (Among its many assets, Hue claims to have Vietnam's most beautiful women.)

Just beyond the second bridge are two of the city's top hotels, the Century Riverside Inn and the Huong Giang. I was booked into the newer Century Riverside. The spacious and spotless second-floor room I was shown to came as a shock after the cramped, frayed quarters on the train: My *bathtub* was bigger than the bed I'd slept in the night before (and actually more comfortable).

From the sunny veranda outside my room, I looked across the Perfume River to the low line of buildings that fringe the waterfront. Along Tran Hung Dao Street, between the river and the walls of the Citadel, was the two-story Dong Ba Market, Hue's main trading center. A flotilla of sampans was strung out along the shore below the market. Each evening toward sunset, just before the lights of the city come on, those boats become black silhouettes on the crimson flood. The strains of Vietnamese music sometimes drift across the water from the floating

Portal of power: The Citadel's most important entryway was the Noon Gate. In Vietnamese folklore, the emperor is symbolized by the sun, which is tallest at high noon. Beyond the elaborate entrance were the Imperial Enclosure, where the emperor carried out his official duties, and the Forbidden Purple City, reserved for the royal family.

A musician dressed in the costume of Hue's imperial court tunes up his instrument in the Palace of Supreme Harmony, where Nguyen emperors presided from a brilliant red and gold elevated throne. After the 1968 struggle for Hue, in which the Communists murdered at least 3,000 of the city's elite, a U.S. Marine with his M-16 assault rifle sits on the throne.

communities, and as darkness settles over the river, the lights of the sampans become golden pinpoints.

Giang and I crossed to the other side of the river on the way to explore the Citadel, a sprawling testament to the one-time power and glory of Vietnamese royalty. In its flower the Citadel was the Vietnamese equivalent of Beijing's Imperial City. Everything about the place was conceived on a grand scale. Begun in 1804, the capital complex spread over some 1,300 acres. It was enclosed by a 75-foot-wide moat and 20-foot-high stone walls that totaled more than six miles in length.

Inside the main walls of the fortress-city was a second set of walls defining the Imperial Enclosure, a citadel-within-a-citadel, where the emperor conducted his official duties. Within the Imperial

Enclosure was the Forbidden Purple City, where the royal family lived, waited on by eunuchs.

Over the years, the procession of Nguyen emperors who occupied the Citadel saw their power gradually siphoned off by the French. After 1883, the French effectively took control of the royal court. Despite their heavy-handed treatment of the emperors, the French didn't end royal rule in Vietnam. But in their struggle to regain control of their prewar possession after World War II, the French did inflict irreparable damage to the pinnacle of Vietnamese culture: In early 1947, the French attacked the Citadel, destroying the Palace of Audiences, the Thai Temple, and the main entrance to the Forbidden Purple City, and severely damaging other structures of this architectural treasure.

That act of desecration was only a warm-up for the devastation visited on the Citadel 21 years later. In 1968, the tranquility of Hue was shattered by the spectacularly destructive Tet Offensive launched by the Communists. Every American who watched the news coverage of that bloody episode can recall the events: Towns and cities throughout South Vietnam came under surprise attack as Viet Cong and North Vietnamese forces took advantage of the lull in the fighting during the annual celebration of the lunar new year, Vietnam's biggest holiday. In most of the country the offensive was over quickly, with the Communists sustaining heavy losses, estimated at up to 40,000 men. In Hue, however, the fighting dragged on. The Viet Cong banner flew from the Citadel's Flag Tower for over three weeks.

In the battle to recapture Hue, American and South Vietnamese forces blasted the city with artillery, naval bombardment, and repeated air strikes. Together with the Communist rockets that were exploding left and right, the American-South Vietnamese attack left the city in ruins. As many as 10,000 people died—including some 3,000 civilians slaughtered by the Communists. Eighty percent of Hue's 140,000 residents were left homeless. By the time the Communists were driven out, large parts of the Citadel—where two-thirds of the city's dwellings were then located—had been reduced to rubble. The most severely damaged area was the Forbidden Purple City, the former sanctum of the royal family. Gone was the emperor's private palace, along with the residences of the emperor's family and royal concubines—all pounded into oblivion. The very heart of the Nguyen dynasty had been ripped out.

So what is left of the Citadel today? Is there anything beyond a shambles of silent stones? Is the place still worth visiting? UNESCO thinks so: It designated the Citadel a World Heritage Site in 1993 for its cultural significance to mankind. While a visit here is at times an exercise in imagining, of piecing together images from remnant walls, there are still magnificent examples of what the Citadel once

was. Just step inside the intricately detailed Throne Palace or stand before the ornate Royal Library and you can glimpse the former splendor of this not too distant empire.

Comprehending the Citadel is easier if you keep in mind that most of this enormous walled complex is simply made up of neighborhoods—streets lined with homes and shops just like in any other part of the city. People enter and leave the Citadel constant-

ly as they go about their business, though no one can fail to recognize the Citadel's boundaries, for you have to cross one of the bridges over the surrounding zigzag moat and pass through one of the narrow gates in the old stone walls.

What you're in fact visiting after you pay your admission to the Citadel is the Imperial Enclosure, the smaller *royal* citadel within the outer walls of old Hue, and the Forbidden Purple City, the royal enclave within. When Ngoc deposited Giang and me in front of the Imperial Enclosure, a soccer game was going on across the street, at the base of the Flag Tower, a stark black pyramid topped by a tall staff, from which Vietnam's gold-starred red banner limply hung. Just beyond, the Perfume River glided past in a gentle curve. Grouped on either side of the

Children play soccer before the crumbling ramparts of the Citadel, whose ornate architecture (above) speaks of bygone splendor. With the help of donor nations such as Japan, Vietnam is spending close to a million dollars to repair the Palace of Supreme Harmony and Forbidden Purple City, as well as some of the priceless tombs of the Nguyen emperors south of Hue. A jagged shell hole (top) is a somber reminder of the fighting that raged inside the Citadel's walls in 1968.

Flag Tower are nine large ceremonial cannons, cast from items of bronze confiscated by Emperor Gia Long from the Tay Son forces he defeated in establishing his dynasty.

Gia Long's humiliation of his enemies reached greater heights than taking away their bronze ware: He reportedly dispatched one predecessor by having him ripped apart by elephants. In 1802, to commemorate the founding of the new dynasty, Gia Long ordered the excavation of the corpses of two Tay Son kings. Gia Long had the corpses ground to powder and scattered. The kings' skulls, however, he put in prison. The skulls were shackled in separate rooms, and a delegation checked on the "prisoners" once a month. The prison where the Tay Son skulls were interned still exists, in the far northwest corner of

the Citadel—today the home of the Tay Loc elementary school.

Giang and I crossed the wide stone bridge leading to the entrance to the Imperial Enclosure. Lotus plants choked the shallow pools on either side of the bridge. Access to this part of the Citadel where the emperor lived and worked is through the Noon Gate, a schizophrenic structure if ever there was one, half fortress, half frill: Sheer-sided brick and stone ramparts, weathered a motley black, rise up from the water, as forbidding as a prison wall; above this foundation—seeming to float on multiple columns—is a graceful two-tiered pavilion of red and yellow lacquered wood and green and yellow tile, the roof ridges undulating with carved dragons. The gate's upper portion—the Pavilion of Five Phoenixes—was where the emperor issued the lunar calendar each year, and it was here that Emperor Bao Dai proclaimed the end of the Nguyen dynasty, surrendering the 22-pound golden seal of the empire, a treasure whose whereabouts is still unknown.

Beyond the Noon Gate we entered the broad, stone-paved Great Rites Court. Across the way stood a hall with red-lacquered doors and a yellow-tiled roof topped by more writhing dragons—the Palace of Supreme Harmony, or Throne Palace. Emperor Gia Long was crowned inside the Throne Palace in 1806, and this was where he and his successors met twice monthly with top-ranking mandarins to discuss affairs of state. Lesser mandarins assembled in the court outside as they waited to pay homage to the emperor.

In the palace's central chamber, the emperor sat upon an elevated red and gold throne, resplendent in a golden robe girdled with a belt of jade and wearing a crown decorated with dragon designs. The Throne Palace's glory—and paint—are a little faded now, but the fact that the building preserves even a semblance of its former splendor is due to a major effort to repair the damage done by shelling in 1968.

At the rear of the Throne Palace lies a courtyard containing the Halls of the Mandarins, pavilions in

The shimmering Perfume River bisects Hue, long regarded as the country's cultural capital. In 1993, UNESCO designated the Citadel as a World Heritage Site. Present-day Hue is built on the remnants of another citadel-city, Phu Xuan, which was founded in 1687 and became the capital of the southern part of Vietnam.

which officials made themselves presentable prior to court ceremonies. The pavilion on the left now houses a souvenir shop, where I bought a guidebook to the Citadel. Nearby was a room containing a throne mounted on a red and gold dais; for two dollars anyone could don imperial garb and have their picture taken sitting there like some ersatz emperor—a genuinely silly prospect for a Westerner but something Vietnamese visitors were taking great pleasure in.

Beyond the Halls of the Mandarins was the saddest spectacle in the Citadel—the rubble-strewn field that now occupies most of the grounds of the Forbidden Purple City. As the sun poured down on the open meadow, I wandered among the foundations of the palaces where the emperor and his family had once lived. Plots of vegetables were growing where the emperor had dallied with his concubines. Women in conical hats tugged at weeds among the plantings. Toward the back of the compound were the remains of an expansive outdoor stage of stone, where royal entertainments had been held. I climbed the steps to the stage, now a pitted, weed-grown ruin. From there the view extended all the way back to the Halls of the Mandarins area, several score yards away—there was nothing left between.

AMONG THE FALLEN EMPERORS

Scattered across the countryside south of Hue are the royal tombs of the Nguyen dynasty emperors. Most were planned or even built by the rulers they honor, and they all share a number of characteristics: a courtyard with statues of mandarins paying tribute to the emperor; a stele pavilion holding stone tablets detailing the emperor's virtues and accomplishments (both real and imagined); and a temple for the worship of the emperor and his empress. The sepulcher itself is usually of a style reflecting the personality of the emperor.

The three most interesting tombs are those of Gia Long's son Minh Mang, who ruled from 1820 to 1840; the handsomely landscaped tomb of Tu Duc, who ruled from 1848 to 1883; and the garish, mosaic-encrusted tomb of Khai Dinh, ruler from 1916 to 1925. I planned to set out for the tomb of Minh Mang in the early morning, traveling on the Perfume River—a boat trip of a little over an hour.

At a landing not far from my hotel, I hired a dragon boat, one of the brightly painted barges named for their carved figureheads. For $15, the captain and his young son would ferry Giang and me downriver, ensconced on benches under an awning in the bow and plied with semicold Pepsi-Colas.

After casting off, we skirted the shore for a short distance, passing an inlet ringed with sampans. Many of the vessels had small Buddhist altars on their roofs, some with joss sticks smoldering in incense holders. A communal TV antenna was attached to a post sticking up from the water, with wires leading to several adjacent sampans. I had an incongruous vision of these people huddled around their sets at night watching *Bonanza*.

Our boat eased away from the bank, and soon we were cruising down the center of the Perfume River, at this point several hundred yards wide. Unlike the turgid waters of the Red River up north, the water here was surprisingly clear, a bottle green—thanks in part to the river's sandy bed. That sand provides a livelihood for any number of Hue families: We passed sampans heaped with river sand, dredged from the bottom by divers using shallow pans. The divers, many of them teenage boys or girls, pile the sand so high that only three or four inches of freeboard remain. The families then up anchor and haul their cargo into Hue, where the sand is sold for use in construction.

It was pleasant to be out on the river before the heat of the day. A cool breeze came off the water as we scooted along. It felt as if we were part of a primitivist painting, executed in bold strokes of emerald and blue—the glassy green water stretching ahead, the riverbanks billowing with plant life, a cloudless sky knitting the horizons.

About 20 minutes into the trip, we stopped to visit the Thien Mu Pagoda, which crowns a hillside on the north bank of the river a couple of miles west of the city—overlooking a scene that a Hollywood set designer might have conceived of as the epitome of the Orient a century ago. The river stretched away to the west, winding out of sight between lush green gardens hugging the shore. In that same direction, ranks of low blue mountains rippled away to the horizon. It was as pure and peaceful a slice of pastoral Vietnam as you're likely to see.

At the top of the flight of steps leading to the pagoda, two Buddhist novices were sweeping the grounds with palm-frond brooms, their young faces as serene as a still mountain lake. Thien Mu was founded in 1601, and the current pagoda—built in 1844—has become a symbol of Hue, an icon as famous in Vietnam as Pisa's canted tower is in the West. Likenesses of the redbrick structure appear on everything from T-shirts to teacups. Some 70 feet in height, the pagoda consists of seven octagonal tiers, each successive layer a bit smaller than the last—a skinny, precariously tall wedding cake.

Over the years, Thien Mu has served as more than tourist icon. In the 1960s, the pagoda was the symbol of Buddhist protests against the Diem regime. South Vietnam's Catholic-dominated

U.S. Marines riding atop an M-48 tank cover their ears as the tank's 90mm gun fires into the jungle along a road southwest of Hue during the 1968 Tet Offensive

Sentinels for a slumbering emperor, rows of mandarin statues guard the gaudy, weathered tomb of Emperor Khai Dinh, who ruled Vietnam from 1916 to 1925. Unlike the other Nguyen dynasty tombs at Hue, Khai Dinh's final resting place is a blend of Vietnamese and European architecture. Some of the mandarins even have European features.

government had a history of persecuting Buddhists, and in response, one of the monks of Thien Mu undertook a form of protest that shocked the world. On June 11, 1963, a 66-year-old monk named Thich Quang Duc had a fellow monk douse him with gasoline in a busy Saigon street. He then set himself afire. The grisly scene was photographed by Associated Press correspondent Malcolm Browne. The government's subsequent crackdown on the Buddhists led

Ao dai-clad visitor graces the majestic tomb of Tu Duc, set amidst a grove of pines and frangipani trees. Tu Duc ruled Vietnam between 1848 and 1883, the longest reign of any Nguyen dynasty emperor. Legend holds that Tu Duc would sit among his scores of concubines in the serenity of Xung Khiem Pavilion (above) and write or recite poetry.

to the evaporation of U.S. support for President Diem.

Behind the main sanctuary at Thien Mu, which contained a large gold-colored laughing Buddha, I came upon a curious sight—an old blue Austin motorcar, sitting up on blocks in an open garage. A fading photograph was attached to the car's windshield. It was a copy of Malcolm Browne's picture showing Thich Quang Duc's self-immolation. The photograph had been taken just moments after the fire was lit; flames were leaping several feet in the air. In the middle of this inferno sat the monk, his face registering a strange repose. A sign on the Austin announced that it was this vehicle that had borne Thich Quang Duc to Saigon.

Nearby, in the peaceful garden behind the sanctuary, the monks were tending their vegetables,

oblivious to visitors. During the protest over Diem's repression, some 30 monks and nuns had burned themselves to death. It was hard to fathom the surety of faith that would allow these gentle acolytes to undertake a sacrifice so horrible in nature.

On the boat again, I found each river mile carrying me further back in time. Scenes of unchanging Vietnam kept materializing on either shore. We passed clutches of women doing laundry at river's edge, and bathers with sudsed-up hair standing waist-deep in the water. Farmers in shorts and conical hats tended their gardens with slow, purposeful movements. Now and then we passed fishermen hauling up submerged bamboo traps to check on their catch. Everything was utterly peaceful, the faultless skies and quiet water, the tranquil, unhurried lives displayed along the shorelines. Then suddenly—much too soon—we were easing up to the bank next to the pathway that leads to Minh Mang's tomb.

Approaching the tomb, we came upon a young Vietnamese man taking a photograph of his sweetheart. The girl sat on the paved courtyard in front of the peeling reddish plaster walls of the entry gate, her long hair draped across one shoulder. The lustrous yellow silk of her ao dai stood out sharply from the old gray stones. A profusion of greenery framed the scene. That set piece of everlasting stone, the self-renewing fecundity of nature, and the evanescent beauty of the girl spoke volumes about this land that has seen so much turmoil and grief. Always there, against the backdrop of war or disaster, you can sense the lengthy lineage of Vietnam, its land and its people, extending backward and forward, the present in fragile equipoise between.

Inside the entryway, I found Minh Mang's tomb to be grand though not gaudy—a balanced, linear arrangement. At the rear of the honor courtyard, three staircases lead to the stele pavilion, after which comes a succession of three terraces leading to the temple dedicated to the emperor and his wife. Beyond the temple, three stone bridges cross the

Lake of Impeccable Clarity. Another three terraces lead to a pavilion from which you can look across the crescent-shaped Lake of the New Moon to Minh Mang's burial place—a large earthen dome enclosed by a circular stone wall and covered with shrubs and pines.

After the architectural pomp leading up to it, this natural sepulcher comes as a surprise. I wondered what sort of man would choose for himself such an unassuming resting place. You couldn't help concluding that Minh Mang was certain enough of his place in Vietnamese history that he didn't need to indulge in self-glorification. He was, after all, one of the last emperors to rule a truly independent Vietnam. I could feel the force of the man's personality reach out across the years.

We walked down to the foot of the bridge that crosses the Lake of the New Moon. Lily pads covered the surface of the lake. Next to the water stood a tree resembling a magnolia, a *su* tree Giang called it. Its fragrant white blossoms littered the paving where we stood. Doves cooed in the tree. Several Vietnamese tourists sauntered toward us across the bridge, the women dressed in their Sunday-best ao dai. (According to Giang, the ao dai was first worn in the time of Minh Mang.) The group paused at the foot of the bridge. One of the men stepped forward and began taking his companions' picture, with the sepulcher in the background.

"The Vietnamese like to have their picture taken here," Giang said. "Minh Mang was a patriot, you see."

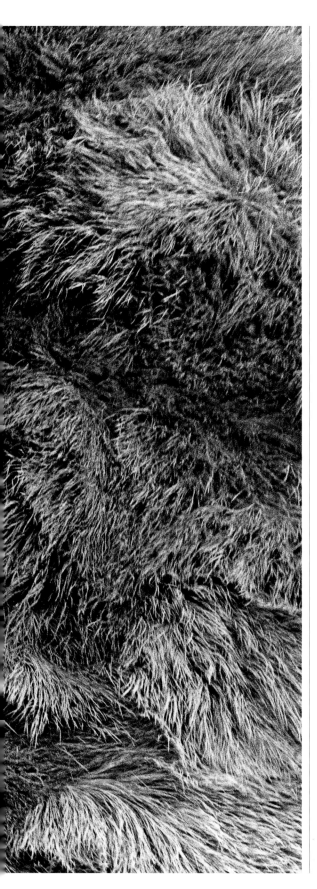

NIGHT ON THE RIVER OF PERFUMES

Giang spoke of another patriot as we drove past a two-story white structure directly across the river from the Citadel's Flag Tower. "That was where Ho Chi Minh went to school," my young guide noted casually, "the Quoc Hoc Secondary School."

I'd read about Quoc Hoc, once one of the most famous secondary schools in Vietnam, attended by sons of the well connected. Not only Ho studied there, but also his future commander-in-chief Vo Nguyen Giap and future North Vietnamese prime minister Pham Van Dong. It's perhaps not surprising that none of the Communist leaders of Vietnam were members of the proletariat, but the irony is that they were attending a school run by the father of Ngo Dinh Diem, the future president of South Vietnam, who was also a student there. The four later-to-be-famous figures had been students at different times, so there was no wrestling in the aisles or schoolyard brawls among them. Their political philosophies would hardly have been mature anyway, though Ho did display his sympathies for the Vietnamese peasants by supporting a local farmers' protest in 1908.

Today's Quoc Hoc school is no longer in the business of turning out political firebrands. It's been converted to a coeducational high school teaching vocational subjects. Just as well. Vietnam could do with more good auto mechanics and electricians and fewer party diehards.

By the time Ngoc dropped me back at my hotel it was time to make plans for the evening. I'd already taken my obligatory pedicab ride around Hue the night before, rolling across Phu Xuan Bridge in the darkness, the Citadel's Flag Tower lit up like a Christmas tree off to the left. On quiet side streets, parents sat on chairs pulled onto the sidewalks, their children scampering around them. Pairs of bicyclists rode leisurely past my pedicab, chatting and joking, sometimes holding hands, seemingly on their way to no place in particular. The shops all around were full of goods. The feeling of contentment was pervasive.

At the Citadel, the pedicab driver had rung his

Making a surprise attack on a Viet Cong stronghold, infantrymen of the 1st Marine Division slog through five-foot-high elephant grass in November 1968. Earlier that year the division fought in the Battle of Hue.

bell as we'd passed through the gate of the old city, the *jing-jing* echoing off the stones of the narrow passageway. Beyond the gate we'd glided through a park where dozens of lovers sat on benches and folding chairs, clinging to one another in absolute darkness, as motionless as statuary, utterly silent. It was at that moment that I'd felt the real magic of Hue.

And now, I decided, what better way to end my stay here than with an evening cruise on the Perfume River? At the hotel's activity desk, I chartered a golden-prowed dragon boat, along with a four-piece ensemble to perform traditional songs of Hue.

Giang and I met the boat at the dock in front of the hotel just as the lights of town were flickering on. The 30-foot craft was powered by a single oar in the rear, so no engine noise would interfere with the music. We clambered down into the passenger compartment, which had a low roof and open windows along each side. A number of lanterns filled the compartment with a warm yellow glow. There were no chairs or benches, merely rush mats covering the floor. Already seated were the four musicians, three women and a man, each in an ao dai—one woman in pale blue, one in yellow, one in apricot, and the man in dark blue. They bowed as we removed our shoes and tucked our legs beneath us on the floor.

As the boatman shoved the barge away from the dock, the musicians launched into a sprightly melody. The man was playing a *dan nguyet*, the long-necked, two-stringed moon-lute. A 16-stringed zither was played with nimble ease by the woman in the yellow ao dai. The two other women were singers, though they added percussion notes from time to time with clacking teacups and wooden sticks.

After the first song, one of the performers explained what the words conveyed. It was a song to welcome guests to Hue and praise the beauty of the city. The group performed one song that told of two

Tucked away in the Thien Mu Pagoda at Hue (opposite) is the Austin motorcar that carried monk Thich Quang Duc to his 1963 self-immolation in Saigon (above)—a protest against the persecution of Buddhists by the American-backed government of South Vietnam. Malcolm Browne of the Associated Press captured the scene in this photograph that was published around the world.

lovers who were separated when the man had to go away to war; the woman is sad, lovesick. Another song spoke about the joy of a native of Hue returning home after an absence. The hoofbeats of the traveler's horse were wondrously rendered with a pair of teacups by one of the singers. During each of the songs, I followed the long, elegant fingers of the zither player. They fluttered over the strings of her instrument, sometimes strumming, sometimes plucking, sometimes hammering out the notes.

I quickly lost track of the time as we drifted through the darkness in our little capsule, the music rippling out into the night, the lights of the city glittering on the river. After the musicians had performed several songs, they put aside their instruments for a moment and began lighting candles inside a number of square-shaped lanterns made of colored construction paper. The flames showed through the sides of the lanterns, glowing in pale rose, soft lemon, aqua. One of the singers handed me a lantern, speaking to me in Vietnamese.

"She says you should put it on the water," Giang explained. I leaned out the open window and placed the floating lantern on the water while the woman continued speaking. "This is what the emperor did when he traveled by boat," Giang interpreted. "It was a symbol of his desire to spread wealth and happiness to his people. You are supposed to make a wish when you place one on the water."

The woman kept handing me the lanterns until I'd launched every one, a dozen in all. Afterward, the musicians returned to their places and resumed their playing. I watched the lanterns trailing slowly away in our wake, a line of glimmering pastel beacons bobbing gently on the black water.

Twelve wishes in Hue. A man could go crazy with the prospect.

PASS OF THE OCEAN CLOUDS

Though the road between Hue and Danang covers only about 70 miles, it takes more than three hours to traverse it. Between those cities, National Highway 1

follows a tortuous route through an east-west spur of the Truong Son Mountains. Cutting all the way across Vietnam's skinny midsection, the mountains here form a barrier that divides the country climatically. North of the mountains the weather is cooler, with frequent typhoons and floods, while to the south the weather remains tropical year-round.

That east-west mountain barrier divides Vietnam in one other significant way. Facing typically cold winters and other harsh conditions, northern inhabitants have evolved a temperament much like that of a frugal New Englander—cautious, straight-laced, eternally prudent. Southerners, able nearly to live off the fat of the land, are a more open and easy-going people, more hot-blooded than their northern kin. Even the food in the north tends to be more con-

servative, the flavors less fiery than in the south.

We drove out of Hue with the golden light of morning spilling across the awakening countryside. A short distance from town we came upon one of those ghostly reminders of America's prior investment in Vietnam—the remains of the Phu Bai Marine air base, still in use as a civilian airport. We passed buildings in various stages of dilapidation, an assortment of tired-looking Quonset huts and maintenance sheds and operations centers. The structures appeared to be slowly settling into the sandy ground, weighed down by time and the elements.

Those relics of war were quickly behind us, and we were rolling on through miles of paddy country, green and level fields butting up against a mass of inland mountains off to our right. The railroad runs

Following pages: Nestled against a spur of the Truong Son Mountains, the palm-shaded fishing village of Lang Co lies between a turquoise lagoon and the South China Sea. South of Lang Co, National Highway 1 climbs to Hai Van Pass, the Pass of the Ocean Clouds, on the way to Danang.

alongside the highway here. Before long both asphalt and steel were edging around a large lagoon, identified as Dam Cau Hai on my map. A couple of dusty towns came and went, and then we were driving out over the water on a long spit of sand, a blue-green lagoon to our right and the South China Sea to our left. Small fishing boats flecked the water on either side of the road.

It was mid-morning when we stopped for a rest in the fishing village of Lang Co, at the tip of the spit we'd been traveling on. A string of fishermen's shanties spread out along the road beneath a canopy of coconut palms. There was an unpretentious hotel and a few beach houses for rent. In the scattering of small cafés you could indulge in the local seafood. Ngoc pulled up at a humble eatery nestled among the trees in back of the beach. We sat down outside and ordered cold sodas. Inevitably, we were quickly surrounded by children and peddlers. Ngoc bought a bag of nuts and began munching away. For some reason, Giang chose that moment to tell me that Ngoc had four children of his own, but that by law only two were permitted to be covered by "social welfare." I don't think Ngoc understood enough English to know precisely what Giang was saying about him, but he smiled anyway. Ngoc's front teeth were edged with gold.

I finished my drink and took a stroll down a sandy path leading to the beach. We were in the heat of the day by now, and hardly anyone was to be seen, though I doubt that at its busiest the beach here ever sees more than a handful of people at a time. Toward the south end of town, a spidery bridge tethered the

Bamboo fishing boat rests on Danang's China Beach, not far from where U.S. Marines splashed ashore on March 8, 1965. By 1966, troops of the 3rd Marine Division routinely patrolled South China Sea beaches atop amphibious tractors. More Marines stormed ashore south of the DMZ (top) in a 1967 search for North Vietnamese troops.

Bound for bountiful fishing grounds, a fisherman fights the pounding surf off China Beach. The day's catch is for sale at a market along the Han River in Danang. Pristine China Beach was a rest and recreation area for American servicemen and women during the Vietnam War. Today developers hope to turn it into a posh resort.

skinny peninsula to the mainland, where the road curled into the mountains that reared up out of the sea. That was where we were heading. That twisting, climbing section of Highway 1 would lead us to Hai Van Pass, the Pass of the Ocean Clouds. (The train chickened out here; it continued to hug the shoreline, ducking in and out of tunnels on its way around the mountains.)

A few minutes later our trusty Peugeot—its transmission whining—labored up the road I'd seen from the beach. At Giang's suggestion, we stopped on a wide curve that presented a scenic overlook. As soon as I got out of the car I recognized the view—it was a Kodak spot, the vantage point from which all the photos of Lang Co that you see in guidebooks are taken. During my travels in Vietnam I encountered

many scenes of surpassing beauty, but at Lang Co, the setting was nearly perfect. The narrow peninsula's pale, virginal beaches were lapped on either side by the turquoise waters of the lagoon and sea, and beyond the lagoon, the brawny, emerald-clad mountains marched away to the north in an irregular procession.

Just below us, the little fishing village drowsed in the sunshine, the stark white spire of its old Catholic church poking up from the trees. If a beachfront paradise exists in Vietnam, then surely this is it. Lang Co was one of those lonely outposts where a handful of people quietly go about their lives surrounded by nature extravagant and pure. You wonder if such people have any sense of the sublime beauty of what, to them, is just their everyday surroundings.

I pondered how much longer Lang Co would retain its peaceable air; someday that venerable church steeple down there will likely be lost among the glitter of resort hotels.

I heard a commotion behind me. Three child peddlers came scuttling across the road, holding trays of goods and shouting, "You buy, you buy." I'd grown so used to saying no—no to trinkets, gum, postcards, headache salve, what have you—that I almost failed to notice the antique silver coin one girl held out. I took the coin to examine. It was the size and heft of a silver dollar. On one side were the words "Indo-Chine Française Piastre de Commerce." On the other a female figure sat above the date, 1896.

It dawned on me that what this girl was actually offering was a totem of her country's stormy history over the past one hundred years. During that coin's existence, the Vietnamese had fought the French, the Japanese, the Cambodians, the Chinese, and, of course, the Americans. Who could guess where the coin had been over the years? It might have bought a night's pleasure in a Saigon brothel for a young French soldier, or jingled in the pocket of the rich owner of a rubber plantation in the Central Highlands. It might have paid for opium in Dalat, or rice in the Mekong Delta, or arms for the Viet Minh. And now it had found its way into my hands. I gave the young peddler her asking price, one U.S. dollar, and pocketed the coin. It would be my lucky charm for the remainder of my trip.

Then it was back in the car to continue grinding upward. The elevation of the pass is only a little above 1,600 feet, but when approaching from the north, you climb to that height from sea level over a distance of about ten miles—the reason for the broken-down buses and trucks along the side of the road. There were frequent turnouts with water for overheated vehicles; every one of them we passed was in use. A number of boulders had tumbled onto the highway, and several roadside shrines marked spots where travelers had died.

"Anyone who must drive here at night first stops to pray that they will make it safely," Giang said over his shoulder.

That sounded like a good idea during the daytime, too.

The Peugeot groaned around hairpin turns, often with precipitous drop-offs just beyond the edge of the road. I was glad I wasn't driving—and that Ngoc had made this run so many times before that

he wasn't tempted to do any rubbernecking. When we finally reached the pass, Ngoc pulled over at the small truck stop where drivers can let their engines cool down. Clusters of entrepreneurial youths were busy washing trucks to make a few dong.

A gray, crumbling French pillbox commanded the pass alongside the highway. The Americans had built a low concrete bunker nearby. My guidebook warned not to go tromping around these fortifications; there were supposedly live mortar shells left lying about. I didn't feel like testing the accuracy of the claim, so I stepped over to the roadside near the truck stop to check out the view. A mist hovered over the pass, but the long golden curve of Nam O Beach was still visible far below to the south, and in the distance, the high profile of Monkey Mountain marked the outskirts of Danang, some 20 miles away by road. Straight down the mountainside, trucks were crawling their way upward like ponderous beetles.

As I jotted a few notes, the usual vendors began homing in on me, three pretty teenage girls this time. After I'd waved off their offers of Pepsi and bottled water, one of the girls shoved her face next to mine and began reading my notes to her friends. The three of them seemed to get a great deal of amusement

Traditional conical hats and bamboo baskets hang on the wall of a home in Hoi An, a riverine town south of Danang. An important port from the 17th century to the 19th, Hoi An today is rapidly becoming a tourist mecca with its slow pace and 200-year-old shops and homes.

from my writing. The girl doing the reading stood back and smiled at me good-naturedly. She seemed to be sizing me up. Suddenly she prodded my stomach. *"Beaucoup bia*—Lots of beer," she pronounced.

Ngoc pulled the cooled-down Peugeot over to the edge of road behind me and beeped the horn. I waved goodbye to the three young vendors, and we immediately began switchbacking down from the heights. Before long we were back on the sandy flats, following the blue curve of Danang Bay toward Monkey Mountain. As we pulled into Danang, I was reminded of the streets of Hanoi—by the incredible piles of odds and ends along the road, the sheer junkiness of things.

Several old U.S. Army trucks were bouncing along the streets, painted in bright colors now,

recycled as commercial vehicles. This had been one of the major U.S. bases in Vietnam, headquarters for I Corps and a major port for the war effort. Historically, Danang figured prominently in the conflicts of this century and the last: It was here in 1965 that the first American combat troops slogged ashore; 118 years earlier, Danang was where French forces began their military assault on Vietnam.

During the American era, Danang rode high on the profits from servicing the immense military machine. After the Americans left, however, Danang's fortunes took a nosedive, hitting bottom in 1975, when, as South Vietnam's defenses crumbled, the city was swept by a firestorm of violence. A million refugees poured into the city overnight. Panicked soldiers and civilians, trying desperately to flee the advancing Communist troops, battled for space aboard the few boats and aircraft available for evacuation. That reign of terror, and the cold-turkey suspension of American largess, left Danang down and very nearly out—a destitute, down-at-the-heels, dispirited place.

Perhaps because of its legacy of capitalism, Danang has been quick to put the country's economic reforms into practice. Vietnam's fourth-largest city (population 600,000) and still one of the country's major ports (it also serves as southern Laos' outlet to the sea), Danang is positioned to become the hub for development along the central coast. The lush Central Highlands at Danang's back and the pristine beaches north and south of the city are certain to attract increasing numbers of tourists. And just down the coast from Danang is Hoi An, a sleepy town that from the 17th century to the 19th was one of Southeast Asia's busiest trading centers, on a par with Macau and Malacca—until its link to the sea, the Thu Bon River, silted up and became too shallow for oceangoing craft, allowing Danang to eclipse it as a port. Hoi An had the distinction of being the first place in Vietnam that Christian missionaries visited. (Back then, the town was known as Faifo.) Among those proselytizing foreigners was

Alexandre de Rhodes, the 17th-century French priest who invented the Latin-based script for the Vietnamese language.

In Hoi An's heyday as a port, ships from around the world sailed up the Thu Bon River, vessels from Holland, Portugal, France, Spain, China, Japan, Thailand—even America. Traders journeyed here to buy silk, porcelain, tea, and other goods. The Chinese and Japanese merchants who called here were forced to lay over from spring until the summer, when the prevailing winds would carry them back home. Eventually the merchants began leaving year-round representatives in Hoi An, the start of the foreign colonies that were to give the town its distinctive architectural flavor. Along the narrow streets, merchants built tiny tile-roofed shops,

warehouses, and homes reminiscent of those in old Hong Kong. The Chinese erected several fine temples and clan halls (Vietnam's ethnic-Chinese still come to Hoi An for celebrations). The ornate Japanese Covered Bridge linked the town's Chinese and Japanese quarters.

Miraculously, Hoi An managed to escape significant damage during the Vietnam War. Parts of it look just as they did two centuries ago, giving the town the feel of a living museum. Inside private homes and shops you can still see beautifully carved wooden interiors, stained dark with time. The pagodas and assembly halls are alive with flamboyant tile work. Best of all, though, is the peacefulness of the place. It has the unhurried, unselfconscious air of a town that doesn't yet realize its own charms.

Passing on knowledge to a generation born since the Vietnam War, a man tutors his grandson on a backstreet in Hoi An. Formerly known as Faifo, the town was the first place in Vietnam visited by Christian missionaries.

Sand and Sanctuaries

Danang's most famous landmark, of course, is China Beach, the miles-long curve of bright white sand and blue, blue water familiar to the thousands of American soldiers who spent R&R here in the '60s and early '70s. China Beach is relatively undeveloped as of now. From the car park of the Non Nuoc Hotel, I walked past a cluster of changing rooms to an outdoor café nestled in a line of pine trees back of the beach. In either direction along that stretch of sand there were maybe 20 people—a few fishermen, a handful of sunbathers, three child peddlers holding trays of seashells. Off to the north, the green bulk of Monkey Mountain marked the emphatic end of Danang's southern stretch of beaches.

Down by the water I stopped to observe two

Vietnamese newlyweds, still in their finery. They were frisking along at the edge of the surf, the groom with his shoes off and his trousers rolled up to his knees, the barefoot bride daintily holding her gown out of the water. The two were mooning and mugging for a video cameraman who was busy preserving these first moments of marital bliss.

Directly behind China Beach loom the isolated limestone outcrops of the Mountains of the Five Elements, more commonly known as the Marble Mountains. From these five large rock formations— one-time islands—comes the red, white, and blue-green marble used by local carvers for tombstones and the ubiquitous objets d'art for sale at kiosks at the beach, in Danang, and all around the Marble Mountains themselves. (The stony hills also supplied building material for Ho Chi Minh's mausoleum in Hanoi.)

The Marble Mountains happen to be honeycombed with caves, which, during the war, made convenient hiding places for the local Viet Cong. Throughout all the years that American soldiers were resting and recreating at China Beach—lolling about on the sand, surfing, making the acquaintance of the local female population—the VC were vigilantly looking down on them from the heights, taking occasional potshots at their enemies.

But long before the Viet Cong sought shelter here, these caves provided sanctuaries of another sort. Over the centuries, the stone chambers have served as religious shrines, with numerous sacred icons carved into the walls of living rock. When this area was controlled by the Cham people, from the late second century into the 1400s, sanctuaries were dedicated to Hindu gods. Later, Buddhist and Confucian shrines were built. The largest of the five hills, Thuy Son (Water Mountain), contains the best examples of those ancient places of worship. The Vietnamese still make frequent pilgrimages to the sanctuaries of Thuy Son. To see these holy places—and to get an inkling of what China Beach looked like to those wartime cave dwellers—I started climbing the intimidatingly steep stone stairway leading up the mountain.

Along the first part of the stairway, knots of war casualties sat on their haunches, hands outstretched. Passing those clusters of blinded, maimed souls was like negotiating a living version of the Stations of the Cross.

There are supposedly 157 steps on the staircase ascending the mountain. I didn't count, though my legs had turned to rubber by the time I reached the most memorable of the caverns, Huyen Khong Cave. When I stepped inside the shadowy recesses of the cave (a flashlight is a definite asset on this trek), my eye was immediately drawn upward. From several holes in the roof high overhead, shafts of light slanted downward through clouds of joss smoke, illumi-

nating a large sculpture of Buddha carved high on one wall. There were also shrines to Confucius, and several inscriptions had been hewn into the rock.

During the war the VC had used this large, gloomy chamber as a field hospital. I shuffled around the gritty floor of the cave, thinking about what it must have been like to lie here wounded. It couldn't have been a very sanitary medical facility, but the inspiring panoply of religious figures that a soldier would have seen from his cot must have been some comfort. On the wall of the cavern was a plaque dedicated to the Women's Artillery Group, whose members in 1972 managed to destroy 19 Marine aircraft parked on the field at the base of the mountains. That testimonial seemed out of place amid the spiritual surroundings, but then it's legitimately part of the history of this ancient sanctum.

U.S. infantrymen sweep the lush coastal plains, riding to war in workhorse UH-1 Huey helicopters. Interdicting North Vietnamese infiltration was a challenge in I Corps, the five northernmost provinces of South Vietnam, which took in the cities of Hue and Danang. Napalm (above) was one effective weapon. The incendiary bombs terrified Communist ground troops, but the horrific effects of napalm touched a raw nerve with the American public, and its use in Vietnam became increasingly controversial.

From Huyen Khong Cave I stepped out into the piercing sunshine and followed the pathway to the Linh Ong Pagoda. Crouched against the side of the mountain, the recently rebuilt sanctuary is fronted by attractive grounds. The shady orchid garden is a restful spot from which to look out over the sea. Unlike the dusty, rock-carved sanctuary of Huyen Khong Cave, everything here was out in the open, washed by the sun, as clean and bright as a porcelain sink. There was a large white Buddha outside the ornate new pagoda. Another figure sported a monstrous, Mick Jaggeresque tongue.

I marshaled my energy for an assault on the billy-goat pathway leading up to the Vong Hai Da scenic overlook, a nearby promontory affording an unobstructed view of China Beach and the South China Sea. A few minutes later I stood on the rocky ramparts, gazing down at the slumberous sands lapped by the gentle surf. There were a number of good-size boulders around the overlook, convenient hiding places for those Viet Cong snipers. I wondered what a Vietnamese guerrilla must have thought,

seeing his enemies scampering around in their
skivvies. I tried to picture what an American soldier
would have made of the situation if the tables had
been reversed. Would the Viet Cong have been
humanized by watching them at play? Not likely.

A MUSEUM FOR THE AGES

In downtown Danang, I checked into the aptly
named Modern Hotel on Bach Dang Street. The
hotel was preternaturally spotless, all polished tile
and dazzling whitewash inside and out. My second-
floor room had a fine view of the Han River directly
below. Out on the street, I walked south along the
river toward the city's most noteworthy sight
(arguably its only noteworthy sight), a pale yellow
stucco building that sits in a little tree-shaded park
on the banks of the Han just four blocks away.
Inside that understated one-story structure, some
300 sandstone or terra-cotta sculptures record the
remarkable artistry of the kingdom of Champa,
which dominated this region from the late second
century to the 15th.

Danang's renowned Cham Museum was
founded under the French in 1915, and it had to
be enlarged in 1936 to accommodate the growing
collection. The museum survived 30 years of modern warfare, though not without abuse. South Vietnamese soldiers once slung their hammocks between
the priceless, thousand-year-old stone carvings.
During the French years, when Danang was known
as Tourane, many Cham treasures were shipped out
of the country to galleries or private collectors. Still,
the specimens preserved here represent the finest
gathering of these works anywhere.

The oldest artwork in the museum dates from
the seventh century. Spread out among the four
large rooms of the open-air gallery—surprisingly
vulnerable to wind and rain—are any number of
sculptures of the female breast, representing the
Cham goddess Uroja. Stone phallic symbols,
along with depictions of sensual goddesses and
meditative images of Shiva, Brahma, and Vishnu,

*Army artillerymen at Firebase
Tomahawk pound North Vietnamese
positions. U.S. bases were shelled just as
mercilessly. At I Corps headquarters in
Danang, Viet Cong rockets and mortars
destroyed 75 million dollars worth of
aircraft in 1967.*

*Rain-laden clouds of the summer
monsoon gather over the Truong Son
Mountains between Hoi An and
Danang. In back of China Beach, five
cave-pocked limestone peaks called the
Marble Mountains harbored Viet Cong
guerrillas during the Vietnam War—
and religious sanctuaries centuries
before that.*

Sampans negotiate Hoi An's Thu Bon River, a waterway that silted up in the late 19th century and became too shallow for large trading vessels, allowing Danang to steal away the commerce of the venerable port. Local farmers still sell their rice and fresh produce at the busy market along Hoi An's waterfront.

confirm the influence of Hinduism on the Chams.

Standing among a display of animal sculptures done between the 12th and 14th centuries, I chuckled at imaginative sea monsters with great bulging eyes, and a chubby figure with the head of an elephant and the body of a lion. I was intrigued by the goddess Uma, whose four arms seemed ready to entwine me if I stepped a bit closer. And there were gods with such infectious grins that they made me hanker to know more about a people who would invest their religious icons with such expressions of boundless joy. The figure I found myself most taken with was a slender dancing girl wearing a scanty costume and a demure smile. The tenth-century sandstone rendering of Apsaras—captured in midstep, her arms and legs curving gracefully—

seemed to make cold stone spring to life.

Evidence of the Cham kingdom still exists all over central and southern Vietnam, in the many vine-encrusted orange-brick towers jutting up around the countryside. Though heavily damaged during the Vietnam War, the finest grouping of Cham towers is at My Son, in a remote valley 37 miles southwest of Danang. To the seafaring, piratical Chams, these gracefully tapering brick towers were the embodiment of their religious beliefs.

If you wish, you can make an effort to sort out the many styles and periods represented by the displays in the Cham Museum, but I wouldn't recommend it—unless you think you can keep the Tra Kieu, An My, My Son, Dong Duong, Khuong My, Chanh Lo, Thap Mam, and Yang Mum styles all straight. I found it far better just to wander from room to room, marveling at the exuberant originality of works rendered with such passion by those artists of long ago.

Toward the end of my visit, I took a seat on one of the benches in the small circular courtyard in front of the museum, across from a group of teenage schoolgirls who sat clustered together like doves on a sill. Dressed in white ao dai, the girls were having their picture taken. The gnarled black limbs of a magnolia tree arched above the girls' heads, the tree's fragrant white blossoms vivid among its waxy green leaves. The scene constituted one of those galvanizing tableaus that I witnessed in this country from time to time. The ethereal beauty of those white-clad girls so perfectly echoed the delicate beauty of the tree's white flowers that for an instant they seemed one and the same, products of the same nurturing soil.

Back at my hotel that evening, I hailed a pedicab rolling down Bach Dang Street. I needed to put Danang to the after-dinner-spin-around-town test. But as we glided up and down the streets of the city, I was frankly disappointed. While Danang may have an attractive setting, with the mountains in the distance and gorgeous beaches all around, the center city is a maze of shabby, crowded streets where people seem preoccupied and not overly friendly.

Upstairs in my room, I flipped on the TV. More rocking Hindus on Channel "V." I tried another station—a roomful of Vietnamese aerobic dancers were bounding about in tights. I switched off the set. For a few moments before turning in, I gazed out the window at the black waters of the Han River.

Early the next morning I was awakened by the sun cresting the horizon. I'd neglected to close the curtains the night before. When I got up to pull the curtains, I saw that the Han River had been transformed into a molten flow. Two inky silhouettes were rowing their ebony sampan across the flaming waters. Down in the street outside the hotel, joggers were padding along, the rubber soles of their shoes softly whapping the pavement.

CHAPTER 4

The Emperor's Sporting Grounds: Nha Trang and Dalat

FLYING TO Nha Trang, we would follow the curve of the central coast below Danang for 335 miles. Shortly after our new ATR plane was airborne, there were glimpses of cloud-fringed mountains off to the right: the Truong Son Range.

As we sped southward between the mountains and the sea, the throaty roar of the turboprops in my ears, I remembered an earlier flight I'd made to Nha Trang—aboard a bulbous-nosed, sow-bellied C-130 out of Saigon. I couldn't avoid the thought that I wouldn't be returning to this coastal city if an unknown Viet Cong artilleryman had aimed his rocket launcher two degrees to the left one sweaty March night in 1971—the exclamation point to my very first day in Nha Trang.

That previous flight had taken me to Nha Trang's Vietnamese Naval Training Center, where my assignment had been to document the effort to prepare the South Vietnamese for the hundreds of boats and ships being turned over to them under President Nixon's Vietnamization program. I hadn't seen much of the city back then; about all I could recall was huddling inside a bunker listening to the thump of outgoing artillery and watching flares light up the sky. Now I'd get to see Nha Trang for what it is today—one of Vietnam's most appealing destinations. Its spectacular setting, with chains of green mountains running down to a turquoise sea, and its Po Nagar Cham towers, regarded as some of the country's finest, have transformed Nha Trang from a quiet fishing town into a tourist hot spot.

Reaching Nha Trang, we dipped down over the mountains and made our landing near the sea. Outside the terminal, my third and final driver was waiting, a slight, taciturn man

Young women in ao dai huddle on a shady bench in the city of Nha Trang, along Vietnam's south-central coast. A U.S. military logistical base and naval training center during the Vietnam War, Nha Trang is now a fast-growing tropical resort.

Fisherman at Qui Nhon mends the giant net he will lower into the placid waters of the South China Sea. All along the central Vietnamese coast, bountiful marine life and calm seas much of the year support a large fishing industry.

named Binh. He was driving a late model gray Hyundai van, an eight-seater in which I ended up riding alone in the rear like a Middle Eastern potentate. Whenever Binh put the van into reverse, a warning device beneath the rear of the vehicle played a merry rendition of "It's A Small World After All."

As we left the airport and headed north along the ocean on Tran Phu Street, I saw immediately how completely I'd failed to notice the beauty of Nha Trang when I was here before. Between those muscular green mountains and a shallow sea of startling hue and clarity lay one of the loveliest beaches I'd ever seen, an arc of white sand that was prettier than China Beach, nearly as beautiful as the deserted strip of sand at Lang Co Peninsula. A median of flowers ran down the center of the roadway, which was lined with outdoor cafés and shade-giving palms—even a small park with a Ferris wheel. The wide streets and small-scale buildings gave the city a low, open feel.

We pulled into the courtyard parking area of a hotel that fronted the sea. The Hai Yen Hotel was one of the clean, modern facilities built to accommodate the growing tourist rush. I was given a pleasant seafront room with a large balcony overlooking the courtyard.

The first thing I wanted to do in Nha Trang was to take a peek at how royalty lived. About three miles south of the city center, situated on an arm of land protruding into the sea, is a complex of five villas once owned by Emperor Bao Dai. Up until his exile to France in 1955, the emperor used to come to Nha Trang to enjoy the felicitous climate—cool nights and the briefest of rainy seasons. Built in the 1920s, Bao Dai's seaside getaway perches on three hills affording stellar views of Nha Trang's four-mile beach to the north, Bamboo Island just offshore to the east, and Mieu Island just to the southeast.

Following Bao Dai's tenure, the villas sheltered top-ranking South Vietnamese officials and, after 1975, Vietnam's Communist elite. Today the estate is operated as a hotel—the Cau Da Villas. Anyone can stay here now, nibbling fresh lobster in the hotel's

restaurant, strolling pathways edged with manicured plantings. Down on Bao Dai's private beach, you can swim where the emperor swam and lie beneath the same shady palms where he once lounged. It won't make royalty of you, but when you languidly wave for a fresh coconut drink from the beachside refreshment stand, you just might feel like it.

A narrow asphalt road wound up to the hotel, with a long flight of steps leading to the main house, a handsome two-story structure of pale yellow stucco commanding the highest hill. The villa was framed with gardens and surrounded by palms and evergreens. At the top, I stood outside the house and savored the view of the long, semicircular beach stretching away to the north. The stark white sand reflected the sun with a glaring intensity. Wooden fishing boats bobbed at anchor close to the shore. The turquoise sea graded to a deeper blue that contrasted with the pale, clear sky. The saturated greens of the mountain backdrop looked newly painted. All the colors were so vibrant that they appeared to have been doctored, in the style of a cheesy travel brochure.

I pictured Bao Dai sipping the evening's first martini, a cigarette in hand as he stood out here in the coolness of dusk in his white dinner jacket, watching the lights of Nha Trang twinkling below. On those soft, pleasant evenings, the music from a record player might have wafted across the lawn to where the emperor stood—swoony big band numbers perhaps. Bao Dai would no doubt have turned back inside for a sumptuous dinner, perhaps followed by a few hands of cards. Then would come other diversions. The man was reputed to be one of the great playboys of modern times. I guess that's understandable. Even an emperor needs an avocation, and if conquering your neighbors or ruling your own people is out of reach, you might as well enjoy yourself.

The villa's rooftop balcony offered what was surely the best view in all of Nha Trang. Bao Dai named his quarters "Breeze-Receiving Villa."

Troops deftly vault from a hovering UH-1 Huey helicopter at an "LZ," as such impromptu landing zones were called. In the II Corps combat zone, which took in the mountainous Central Highlands and adjacent lowlands, air transport was vital to rapid troop movement.

He called another house on the estate "Moon-Admiring Villa." The stars would certainly be yours to touch sitting up there at night.

From the villas, we skirted the beach again on the drive to the northern end of town, where we crossed the broad-mouthed Cai River. Nha Trang's picturesque fleet of wooden fishing trawlers, all painted the same deep blue, rode at anchor among the sheltering islands below Xom Bong Bridge. The people of Nha Trang have long made a living from the sea, harvesting a bounty of lobster, shrimp, scallops, and fish from the region's placid blue waters.

Just across the river are Nha Trang's Po Nagar Cham towers, a good substitute for anyone unable to visit the Cham relics at My Son. Four of the original brick towers of Po Nagar still stand. They were built between the 7th and 12th centuries, on a tree-shaded hill that had been used by Hindu worshipers as far back as the second century. To reach the towers, I had to climb a flight of stairs leading past the pillars of a ruined meditation hall, the former entrance to the complex.

At the top, I walked around the four orange-brick towers. The largest, the 75-foot-high North Tower, was the best preserved and most interesting architecturally. Pilasters topped with sharply pointed arches embellished its outside walls. The roof consisted of a series of pyramidal terraces, where bushy green plants sprouted among aged brick sculptures. Removing my shoes inside the tower's vestibule, I stepped into the dim interior chamber. Forests of incense smoldering on the altar gave off pungent, chest-constricting fumes. I couldn't stay inside for more than a few moments. Squinting through my tears, I looked up at the vaulted ceiling, which was blackened from hundreds of years of smoke from burning joss sticks. People still come here to pray and make offerings—Vietnamese and ethnic-Chinese Buddhists as well as Chams. (There are still some 60,000 Cham people in Vietnam, who continue to worship a form of Hinduism, and who still make use of their own script, derived from ancient Sanskrit.)

Outside the tower, visitors were having their pictures taken with two shy Cham girls wrapped in yards of bright cloth.

A few minutes to the north, Hon Chong Promontory—a spit of granite jutting into the sea—offers unexcelled views of the coast to the north and south. A row of refreshment stands perch on a bluff above the promontory's rocky tip. Giang and I eased ourselves into a couple of beach chairs and ordered up some drinks. A constant breeze fluttered the bamboo awning above our heads. Seabirds squawked and wheeled in the wind. Far away to the south, Bao Dai's villas ruled over the town. Down below, Nha Trang's fishing fleet was just now heading out to sea, dozens of boats fanning out like an armada, heading toward the islands on the horizon and beyond, where they

would spend the whole night fishing and return to port in the morning.

When the young waitress returned with our beers, she pointed at the line of mountains to the northwest. "That is Fairy Mountain," she said brightly. "See—her face, and there are her breasts, and there her legs."

There were lots of breasts and legs on display at Nha Trang's renowned municipal beach. All I had to do was cross the street from my hotel to reach the heart of this seaside playground. Directly opposite the Hai Yen, shaded by coconut palms, was one of the clusters of open-air cafés that line the strand. Unlike at China Beach, the beach scene at Nha Trang was a lively one. The resort is particularly popular with the French. White-hulled cruise ships often anchor

Open-air café provides a restful view of the beach at Nha Trang, where the billowing canopy of a parasail buoys up thrill-seekers. Known for its pristine sand and water, Nha Trang has become a popular stop for cruise ships.

offshore, and parasailers now zoom above the crystalline blue waters, dangling like clusters of ripe fruit beneath their neon canopies.

The forecast is that Nha Trang will rival Thailand's Pattaya Beach in years to come. With the increase in tourism, service industries are already on the rise—from the new hotels and restaurants to scuba and snorkeling operations. Caucasian sunbathers were everywhere on the beach, but they

Betting against time, a vendor hauls blocks of ice in a pedicab to roadside restaurants along National Highway 1. Nha Trang's mild climate was enjoyed by Vietnam's last emperor, Bao Dai, until his 1955 exile to France. The complex of five seaside villas he once owned now operates as a hotel, the Cau Da Villas.

Stream of humanity rolls along National Highway 1 at Nha Trang. The city's fleet of bright blue trawlers sails from the protected mouth of the Cai River into the South China Sea to harvest abalone, lobster, prawns, and an assortment of fish for area markets, restaurants, and seafood processing plants.

were nearly outnumbered by the vendors hawking snacks, drinks, and curios.

People were strolling along the esplanade arm in arm, wandering in and out of the cafés for drinks or dinner. Before long the cafés began turning on their lights for the evening, transforming the tourist strip into a carnival midway tucked among the trees, right down to that jolly little Ferris wheel.

A VISIT WITH THE GOOD DOCTOR

There was another place in Nha Trang worthy of a visit, a memorial to a French medical missionary whose dedication to Vietnam—and Nha Trang in particular—earned him a lasting place in the hearts of the Vietnamese. The Yersin Museum honors Dr. Alexandre Yersin, the man who in 1895 founded

Artilleryman of the Army's 7th Battalion, 15th Field Artillery, lugs an eight-inch shell to a firing position near Qui Nhon. Like Nha Trang and Cam Ranh Bay to the south, Qui Nhon became a major military supply port.

Nha Trang's Pasteur Institute, one of several similarly named medical research centers in Vietnam (others were established in Hanoi, Dalat, and Saigon). The goal of these centers was—and is still—to study and eradicate infectious disease.

On the second floor of a back wing of the Pasteur Institute's main building, Dr. Yersin's office and library have been preserved as a museum. It was early morning when Binh pulled up in front of the complex, located on Tran Phu at the northern end of town. Inside the front gate, patients were lined up at the door of the center's yellow stucco clinic, awaiting vaccinations. My guide, a pleasant, middle-aged woman in dark slacks and a loud print blouse, led me through the halls of the two-story main building, where white-coated researchers were at work in anti-

quated, underlit facilities that resembled a junior-high science lab. It was hard to believe that research on modern-day killers such as AIDS was going on in those rooms. Vaccines for diphtheria, typhoid fever, rabies, and other diseases are still manufactured here.

The 26-year-old Swiss founder of this institute had come to Vietnam in 1889 after working for several years as an assistant to Louis Pasteur. Before he left Paris, Dr. Yersin had already made a name for himself in the field of bacteriology, having shared in the discovery of the diphtheria toxin.

Dr. Yersin spent his early years in Vietnam exploring the Central Highlands. He settled in Nha Trang in 1891, and he would spend more than a half-century of his life here. After setting up the local Pasteur Institute, he ministered daily to the medical needs of the Vietnamese, all the while carrying on his research.

I followed my guide up the steps to the Yersin Museum. She and I were the only people here. In the empty, silent library—still used by the institute— Yersin's old medical tomes shared space with current periodicals. We stepped into Yersin's office, where the woman proceeded to enumerate Yersin's many accomplishments during his lengthy residence in Nha Trang.

"Dr. Yersin bring rubber and quinine trees to Vietnam from Brazil and Malaysia," the woman said in a soothing voice. "He set up plantations near Nha Trang. He was first to produce drugs to fight malaria, you see."

The woman indicated a microscope among the inventory of equipment. "In 1894 Dr. Yersin volunteer to go to Hong Kong to help combat an outbreak of bubonic plague. He operate on corpses to find the cause of the disease. In six days he discover the bacterium. He develop serum that save many lives. He was then 30 years old." She rested her hand on the instrument's burnished wooden case. "This was the microscope he use."

I was transfixed by the significance of that device. Here was the very microscope with which the

rat-borne plague bacillus *(Yersinia pestis)* had been isolated—one of the milestone accomplishments of medical history. The instrument seemed to belong in some vaunted hall of honor, yet here it was in this unpretentious museum in Nha Trang—just sitting there for anyone to touch.

There were other artifacts on display that demonstrated the range of Dr. Yersin's interests, including astronomical instruments and a hand-cranked generator that Yersin brought back from Paris in 1900 in order to conduct experiments with electricity. (Yersin also imported the first helicopter to Vietnam and the first motorbike.) A barometer indicated Yersin's scientific interest in weather; the guide explained that the doctor had learned how to forecast typhoons—a benefit to local fishermen—

and that he often studied cloud systems with a telescope from the roof of his home.

At one point the guide showed me a fine old stereopticon, a wonderful Victorian contraption of polished wood and brass fittings. She urged me to look into the eyepiece, where I saw a black-and-white 3-D image of dark-skinned Vietnamese fishermen standing on the beach at Nha Trang. The woman told me to turn the handle on the side of the wooden box, which caused a new image to flip into view, this one a scene of the Nha Trang market in 1900. Slowly cranking the handle, I looked at a series of slides, haunting images of long-dead Vietnamese going about their daily lives.

Dr. Yersin's own hand had once turned this handle, the same hand that had altered history with

GI leads a Viet Cong prisoner to an interrogation center on the Bong Son Plain of the central coast of Vietnam. While pacification was the primary objective of the war effort, U.S. soldiers found it hard to win the hearts and minds of Vietnamese, who could be farmers by day and guerrillas by night.

those pioneering medical discoveries. Yersin himself had made these fragile glass plates. They were each one of a kind, irreplaceable, priceless historical documents. I tried to imagine being allowed—encouraged—to manipulate something this valuable at the Smithsonian. I was tempted to advise the guide that she really shouldn't let visitors operate the device. The very idea that someone could do that seemed quaint, naive even, a demonstration of just how lightly tourism had touched this little museum.

The woman led me back to an area where some of the doctor's personal effects had been relocated from his home, including his clock and his rocking chair. A bookcase was filled with detective novels—works by Dorothy Sayers, Arthur Conan Doyle, and Philip MacDonald. There were also books by Jack London and several romantic novels. (Yersin had never married, so perhaps he had to get his romance vicariously.)

The guide pointed to a small bed. "This is the bed in which Dr. Yersin die," she said. "He still working two days before he die. He make tide chart by looking at the sea with binoculars from his bedroom window. After he die, the Vietnamese put his picture in pagodas to revere him."

The museum had a photograph of Yersin, taken near the end of his long life (he was nearly 80 years old when he died in 1943). The picture showed a bald, white-bearded man with a long, thin face. It was a kind and intelligent face, a bit sad, it seemed. The good doctor is buried outside Nha Trang, on a site he selected himself.

THE CITY OF LOVE

By car, it's around five hours from Nha Trang up to the Central Highlands resort of Dalat. About half of the 130-mile route follows Highway 1, tracing the bulge of the coast all the way south to the city of Phan Rang. For the first part of the drive, we would traverse long stretches of open countryside, passing through a few dusty towns. Mostly I recall distant mountains, vistas of the flat blue sea, and lots of palm

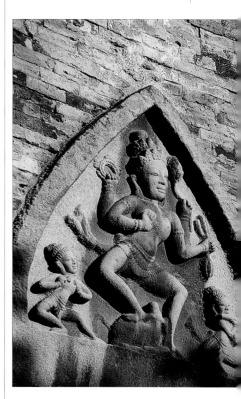

Relics of a vanished empire, Nha Trang's Po Nagar Cham towers were built between the 7th and 12th centuries. Above the entrance to the North Tower, a four-armed Shiva goddess is flanked by musicians. The Hindu-influenced Chams ruled central Vietnam from the late second century to the 15th.

trees. It was unpleasantly hot, so Binh kept the air conditioner howling.

Midway along that portion of our trip we passed Cam Ranh Bay, the major American supply port during the war. Lyndon Johnson visited the troops here on two occasions, encouraging his boys to "nail the coonskin to the wall." Those who know the beaches of Cam Ranh Bay say they're first-rate, although because of the bay's military significance, tourism has yet to visit the area. After 1975, the Soviets maintained their largest naval base outside the USSR at Cam Ranh Bay. Following the collapse of the Soviet Union, that presence has withered away.

At Phan Rang we turned inland from the coast, branching off Highway 1 onto Highway 20. We had to cross an expanse of near-desert-like flatlands before we started rising slowly toward the mountains. A steep, switchbacking climb took us to the top of a pass from which we could see all the way back to the coast, over 30 miles away. This was Ngoan Muc Pass, aptly named Bellevue Pass by the French. There was an old train station here, one of the stops on the cog railway that linked Dalat with Phan Rang from 1928 until 1964, when the line was shut down after repeated attacks by the Viet Cong.

Our ascent had transported us to a new climate. Binh was able to shut off the van's air conditioner, and we opened all the windows. The breeze batting me in the face carried the fresh, spicy fragrance of pines. The trees were all around us, for here at 3,200 feet we'd reached the alpine zone of the Central Highlands, an untropical realm of vertical slopes cut by tumbling streams and frothing waterfalls, with vest-pocket valleys patchworked by plots of vegetables. Some peaks in the region top 7,000 feet.

As pleasant as these pine forests are, plenty of people seem eager to chop them down. Loggers and slash-and-burn farmers have clear-cut entire hillsides, resulting in erosion and the silting of watercourses. The government has fought against deforestation for years—tree-planting projects, which go all the way back to Ho Chi Minh, are part of the

A young woman pauses on the beach at Nha Trang, which drew thousands of American GIs for in-country rest and recreation. The city was spared the heavy shelling that was commonplace at coastal bulwarks such as Danang.

Surrounded by verdant mountains, Nha Trang has been a busy regional port since French colonial days. The sparkling waters beyond the city have lately been discovered by snorkelers and scuba divers.

Infantrymen on a search-and-destroy mission hunt enemy units and supply caches in the Central Highlands, a strategically important region that saw considerable fighting during the Vietnam conflict.

educational curriculum in Vietnam. We passed several billboards along the highway encouraging local woodsmen to spare the trees—a message conveyed to the illiterate (or to visiting foreigners) with drawings of axes with x's through them.

Constituting the southern reaches of the Truong Son Range, the Central Highlands are home to many of Vietnam's ethnic minorities, whom the Vietnamese sometimes refer to as "Moi"—savages—an attitude that reveals why the hill tribes are at the bottom of society in economic and educational status. Montagnards can usually be seen in the marketplace at Dalat, offering their produce and handicrafts for sale. The government would like these semi-nomads to stay put and has encouraged their settlement in permanent villages, some of which lie along

Highway 20. About a dozen miles outside Dalat, we passed a village inhabited by members of the Koho minority. The village's distinguishing feature was a large concrete statue of a rooster, a landmark whose origin and significance even the villagers are uncertain of.

Closer to Dalat, Binh pulled over in front of a busy roadside restaurant. Alongside was the entrance to the Prenn Falls park. Guidebooks tout Prenn Falls as one of the largest and most scenic in the vicinity of Dalat. I followed the pathway through a narrow, pine-filled valley down to the falls. Cascading over a wide lip of rock, they plunged about 50 feet into a circular pool below—which was altogether too small for the fleet of tourist boats tied up along the edge. The water was the color of café au lait, the result of

deforestation upstream. A wooden walkway crossed the pool at the side of the cataract, where a pathway recessed into the rocks led behind the screen of falling water.

Back in Emperor Bao Dai's heyday, the Prenn Falls area—the entire region around Dalat—was a prime hunting ground. Up until the 1950s, big-game hunters from all over were attracted by the Central Highlands' multitude of wild creatures—tigers, leopards, bears, elephants, rhinos, wild boar, deer, several species of wild ox, and birds and monkeys galore. Even Teddy Roosevelt kept a hunting lodge in Dalat for a time.

Too many years of hunting—legal and otherwise—coupled with human encroachment and the devastation of woodlands brought about by the

Vietnam War, have severely reduced the numbers of wild animals throughout the country. Certain species, such as the tapir and the Sumatran rhinoceros, have been wiped out altogether. A spate of new national parks provide at least some protection for the animals and their habitats, although poachers are a problem. The most intriguing news relating to Vietnam's wildlife were two recent discoveries of previously unknown species—a large goat-like animal found in 1992 in the northern part of the country near the border with Laos, and a species of barking deer discovered in the same area in 1994.

From Prenn Falls, we kept climbing toward Dalat. The town lies at 4,800 feet, which explains how it earned one of its two nicknames—the City of Eternal Spring. It's claimed that the temperature in

Rice farmers cultivate their fields along National Highway 19 near An Khe, in the Central Highlands west of Qui Nhon. A plateau at the southern end of the Truong Son Mountains, the Central Highlands are home to many of Vietnam's 54 ethnic minority groups.

Women traders bargain over the price of freshly picked coffee beans in a Ban Me Thuot market. Coffee, now exported to the United States, is the principal crop of the fertile Central Highlands region between Ban Me Thuot and Pleiku.

Woman offers ducks for sale in a market at Ban Me Thuot, one of the least visited areas of Vietnam. The town has the distinction of being the site of one of the final battles of the Vietnam War.

Dalat never drops below 50 degrees in winter or goes above 70 in summer. In this felicitous climate, the chief activities consist of growing flowers and vegetables and playing host to a continual parade of honeymooners—the activity that prompted Dalat's other nickname: the City of Love.

I'd been in Dalat once during the war, on a visit to the Vietnamese Military Academy, where officers for all branches of South Vietnam's armed forces were trained. Now *that* was good duty. This garden spot has been a getaway—first for the French, then for the Vietnamese—ever since it was established as a hill station on the advice of Dr. Alexandre Yersin. Even in the war years, Dalat proved a restful haven: Officials from both South and North Vietnam were said to have spent their holidays here—with the

tacit understanding that no one would be overly inquisitive about the affiliations of their neighbors. (That tale is probably apocryphal, but it makes for a good story.)

Binh drove into a green valley surrounded by pine-covered ridges. As we entered Dalat, here is what greeted us: polychrome flower beds and bright yellow and white chalets clinging to the hillsides, a lively central market and quiet cafés, and a sky blue lake commemorating a 17th-century poet. On the lake, young couples leisurely splashed about in paddleboats shaped like swans, while pony carts clip-clopped past an undulating 18-hole golf course and the luxurious Dalat Palace hotel.

That stately hilltop hotel is the city's finest—and costliest—place to stay, but for your money you get authentic colonial ambiance (the hotel was completed in 1922) and fine French cuisine. You also get one of the best views of that centerpiece lake, from some of the most peaceful grounds anyone could wish for, where neatly clipped grass and flamboyant floral displays slope down toward the water. You can sit for hours in the cool stillness just soaking in the scenery.

I was staying at a less expensive place, the Ngoc Lan Hotel, which has its own view of long, narrow Xuan Huong Lake from a hillside on the western end. The hotel also offers a nitty-gritty prospect on the Dalat business district. Lower down the hillside, a crazy quilt of curbside vegetable sellers spreads north along Nguyen Thi Minh Khai Street toward the central market, their baskets piled with the bounty of the surrounding hills: strawberries, scallions, pineapples, tomatoes, beans, radishes, potatoes, apples, avocados.

Binh drove me down to the opposite end of the lake, to the Dalat Flower Gardens, established in 1966 and renovated in 1985 after having gone to weeds for several years. Inside were well-ordered beds of rich orange soil, where hydrangeas, fuchsias, roses, and lilies bloomed in profusion. There were drooping trees covered with fuzzy red flowers, a pond that mirrored the clouds overhead, and a children's playground with a merry-go-round. (There were also a few pathetic monkeys in cages, looking totally nonplussed as to why they were here.) The cool, damp air smelled of pines and dirt. I sat on one of the park benches and quietly owned everything in sight for several minutes—the only paying customer around. The few Vietnamese I did see surprised me by their attire: Many were wearing sweaters, coats, or scarves. To the Vietnamese, the climate apparently seemed frigid, though I was comfortable sitting there in my shirtsleeves.

I decided to walk back to the hotel, a mile or so away—despite Giang's protestations that it was much too far. A road paralleled the curving northern shore of Xuan Huong Lake. The tall beige spire of the

Dalat Cathedral was visible across the water. I met a steady stream of bicyclists and pedestrians, and several of the popular Dalat pony carts came bobbing along, passengers tittering in back, drivers impassively flicking the rumps of the sturdy little horses with their whips.

On my right for nearly the entire distance along the lakeshore were the 120 rolling acres of the Dalat Pine Lake Golf Club. Built as nine holes in

1920, the course had just been expanded to 18 by a Thai company. The bougainvillea-draped Tudor clubhouse had been refurbished so handsomely that even Bao Dai—who used to play here—would feel at home. No one appeared to be playing today, although guests at the Dalat Palace have access to the course. From the third hole, you can see the smokestack and concrete dome of Vietnam's only nuclear facility, built by the U.S. in 1963 and now used as a research center.

At the lake's western end, I stopped beside the Thanh Thuy Restaurant. Concessionaires were renting the swan-shaped paddleboats that are popular with honeymooners, though business had slowed noticeably, since the breeze was kicking up a chop on the water.

Camouflaged soldier is captured by Army photojournalist Jon Olson, whose portraits of American GIs were widely published. Olson was part of a small band of young military photographers who shared the hardships and horrors of battle with the infantry.

Paratrooper of the 173rd Airborne Brigade cries out to a wounded comrade on bloody Hill 875 at Dak To, where the brigade won a Presidential Unit Citation in November 1967. Army photographer Gordon Gahan, who made the photograph, was decorated for heroism.

IN THE EMPEROR'S BEDROOM

During the reign of Bao Dai, Dalat had served as the emperor's summer capital, and the palatial villa where he lived, southwest of Xuan Huong Lake and the central city, has been preserved as a museum. We drove up through the piney hills on the way there, passing some of the fine chalet-style houses the French built when they occupied Dalat, many set among tall trees and surrounded by bougainvillea and mimosas. A number of villas were for rent.

Bao Dai's belongings still fill the 25-room summer palace he had constructed in 1933. Situated in a grove of pines, the blocky mustard yellow house offers an intimate glimpse of the royal lifestyle. A flat roof and rounded corners gave the villa a streamlined, art deco look. In the formal gardens at the rear of the house, a pathway led past neatly clipped hedges. Pastel roses stood out against the greenery of shrubs in a sunken garden. The late afternoon sun had begun to slant through the tall pines, casting long shadows across the grounds.

A queue of Vietnamese tourists waited outside the front door. As we filed into the house, we were required to remove our shoes; once inside, though, I had to wonder why the curators bothered to enforce the policy: Everywhere, visitors were making themselves right at home, lounging on chairs and sofas, handling the emperor's personal items as if they were their own. The cushions of the sparely elegant '30s-modern furniture were worn slick in places.

In Bao Dai's first-floor office, a man seated behind the emperor's mammoth desk was having his picture taken. He was holding a telephone to his ear and grinning self-consciously. Around the office were reminders of the former occupant. A life-size white bust of Bao Dai sat on a bookcase alongside two smaller busts of his father, Emperor Khai Dinh. Amid the memorabilia were two heavy brass seals, one for royal papers and one for military. Photographs above the fireplace showed a pudgy, oily-looking Bao Dai; his wife, Empress Nam Phuong, a former beauty queen who died of cancer

in 1963; and their oldest son, Crown Prince Bao Long, who now lives in exile in England. (The family included another son as well as three daughters.) For a man of wealth, Bao Dai didn't look particularly happy. Maybe he'd known his emperoring days were numbered when that picture was taken; he'd had warning enough to prudently sock away a fortune in Swiss banks.

In the cavernous reception room, tourists were taking turns sitting at the grand piano to have themselves immortalized on film. Over the fireplace, the horns of a wild buffalo bagged by Bao Dai gleamed dark and menacing. In the dining room close by, visitors milled around a long table that could easily have seated two dozen. Windows stretched from the floor to the lofty ceiling, admitting a nacreous light that

illuminated an engraved glass map of Vietnam given to Bao Dai by some Vietnamese students.

Everything in the house supposedly appeared just as it had during the emperor's residence. The pieces of China and glass collectibles had once known the touch of royal fingers, and that grand piano had reverberated with music fit for an emperor's ear. The only incongruous object was a large portrait of Ho Chi Minh, displayed so that no one could miss the Communist leader's benevolent smile. (You can rent a room here for the night, though with all the people clomping through I wouldn't fancy it.)

On the second floor are the family's large, airy bedrooms, each with a fine view of the grounds. The crown prince's room was done up in royal yellow, and I saw the sleeping quarters of the underling

Taming a wild elephant is a matter of man over beast. Near the Central Highlands village of Ban Don, a member of the M'nong hill tribe plunges the head of a recently captured baby elephant beneath a fast-moving stream to gain the animal's submission. The M'nong use elephants as beasts of burden (opposite).

Tanks and armored personnel carriers protect a U.S. supply convoy moving through the rolling hills of the Central Highlands. From Pleiku, headquarters of the II Corps combat zone, heavy tank units of the 4th Infantry Division and 3rd Brigade of the 25th Infantry Division roamed west toward the Cambodian border.

Men of the M'nong hill tribe, a close-knit group whose surnames are passed down through the female line instead of the male, smoke tobacco through water pipes to celebrate the beginning of the rice harvest at the village of Ban Don.

prince, Bao Thang (who's now living in France, doing a "technical job"), and the beds of princesses Phuong Lien (today working in a French bank), Phuong Dung (an interpreter for the United Nations), and Phuong Mai (she's married to a Frenchman). Empress Nam Phuong's bed chamber was enormous, befitting the daughter of a rich landowner. Bao Dai had a separate and equally grand bedroom; the emperor could step outside on a private balcony for his "breeze-getting" and "moon-watching."

In the "distraction room," the emperor once took his ease at chess or cards, or relaxed in a hammock. Nearby was the parlor where Bao Dai and his family held private gatherings. The emperor and empress sat formally on a semicircular couch, their children arrayed in front of them, the two sons on

one side and the three daughters on the other. It did not appear to be a very intimate arrangement. Maybe they were happy together, maybe not. It did transpire that Bao Dai's wife left him and moved to France before she died. While Bao Dai remained in Vietnam, he staved off loneliness with his favorite royal concubine.

We wound our way back down into town as evening came on. Near my hotel, I stopped at the Artista Restaurant, whose veranda offered a nice view of Xuan Huong Lake. By the time I finished my fried rice with beef and fresh local vegetables, I was hugging my teapot for warmth. Don't let anyone tell you it doesn't get cold at night in Dalat. The people whizzing by on motorbikes were bundled in heavy jackets. One fellow came thundering up the road wearing a Soviet-style fur hat, the ear flaps down and secured beneath his chin.

In the morning, I was up before sunrise, looking out my front window at the shimmering slab of slate that was Xuan Huong Lake. The pine trees were still black silhouettes, the distant hills mere smudges on the gray horizon. Streetlights encircling the lake glowed like multiple moons in the mist-filled dawn, casting long, indistinct reflections on the water. Even at this hour, ghostly figures bore baskets of fruit and vegetables in the streets below. I sat at my window until the emerging light had transmuted the hills from black to green.

After breakfast I took a walk past the central market (wearing a sweater—I could see my breath in the brisk dawn air). A few dark-skinned minority women were congregated at the top of a set of stone steps leading down to the market. They had laid out a selection of brightly colored handwoven blankets for sale. As I stopped to inspect their wares, they watched with a shyness that was touching, conferring in whispers like a convocation of nuns.

We were making an early start this day for Saigon, some 200 miles to the southwest—another drive of about five hours. Once outside of Dalat, we began plunging down steep, pine-covered slopes on

the continuation of Highway 20. For the first half
of the trip, we would remain in the forested highlands, passing a string of minority villages. Some
of the houses were finished with vertical sections
of unpeeled logs, which, together with their second-
story balconies, gave the homes a rustic, Swiss-alpine
look. The women of these villages formed a steady
stream of foot traffic beside the road, stately figures
in long skirts, nearly every one of them bearing a
baby strapped to her back with a cloth sash.

We passed through a succession of fruit-growing
areas, the valleys lined with neat blocks of trees. In
the vicinity of Bao Loc, we drove past tea and coffee
plantations. The tea bushes grew thick on the steep-
est hillsides. Women with baskets stooped among
the plants, plucking the precious leaves. Stands of
mulberry trees, for use in silk production, also
flourished around Bao Loc.

After three hours, the mountains trailed off
into gentle hills then petered out altogether. We were
back in the heat of the flatlands. Bougainvillea hung
thick along the roadside, erupting into bonfires of
pink, orange, and magenta blossoms. Here in the lowlands were tracts of rubber trees, whose lower limbs
had been removed to allow access to the trunks. The
bark on each trunk was scarred repeatedly with deep
slashes, the most recent of which had a metal spout
driven into the tree at the bottom of the cut, to guide
the milky liquid latex into a collecting bowl.

At the crossroads town of Dau Giay, just past
the faded-khaki waters of the huge Tri An reservoir
(source of most of Saigon's electricity), Highway 20
rejoined National Highway 1. Twenty-five miles due
west we crossed the Dong Nai River at Bien Hoa—a
pair of place-names that welled up from my past. We
were entering the nexus of my wartime experience,
the swampy, paddy-and-palm-sprinkled zone surrounding the old southern capital.

Heading southwest out of Bien Hoa on the final
17-mile run to Saigon, we began to pass an inordi-
nate number of Catholic churches. It was as if some
pent-up religious fervor had been unleashed here in

a frenzy of temple-building, a bastion against the godless north. Some of these churches sat so close together that it seemed unlikely each could fill its pews without stealing someone else's parishioners.

Sprinkled among all those churches were dire-looking soup stands and derelict shops and homes, their yards gobbled up by piles of car parts and stacks of bricks. But there was evidence of a nascent prosperity amid all the mildewed stucco and rusted

Dalat's renowned flower gardens draw visitors of all ages. So many newlyweds honeymoon at the mountain resort that it's been called the City of Love. Emperor Bao Dai kept a home in Dalat, his summer capital. The palatial villa is now open as a museum.

Attendant at the sumptuous Dalat Palace hotel unveils a spectacular view of scenic Xuan Huong Lake. A former French hill station and popular resort, Dalat lies at 4,800 feet in the Central Highlands, giving the city perhaps the best weather in Vietnam.

tin—in the legion of billboards advertising a cornucopia of goods: automobile tires, bathroom fixtures, sewing machines, liquor, cellular telephones, Saigon Cola. There were splashy announcements for swank new apartment complexes and locally made Mekong Star sport utility vehicles—even a sign heralding the new San Tap driving range.

The traffic began to swell noticeably the closer we drew to Saigon. Motorbikes, trucks, and jitneys were streaming to and from that as yet invisible metropolis of five million people somewhere to the west. Then off in the distance, high rises started poking above the ragged tops of palm trees. In no time at all we were clattering across the Saigon River bridge, and suddenly, after 24 years, I was back—in the place that today is called Ho Chi Minh City.

CHAPTER 5

In the Belly of the Dragon: Saigon and the South

WHAT ABOUT that name? Ho Chi Minh City. Did anyone actually call the place by that unwieldy moniker? Giang did, but then he was Hanoi born and bred, and the city had carried that label for most of his lifetime. Technically, the metropolitan area is divided into a dozen or so precincts, and the easternmost sector, District 1—the downtown core of commerce and government—is officially known as Saigon. But virtually everyone you meet refers to the entire city by that name. I could never think of it as anything else. Too many memories were bound up in that word, memories as sharp as the smell of burning incense. In my mind's eye, I could still see the street barricades of barrels and barbed wire, the sandbagged entrances to hotels, the makeshift lean-tos of the poor, the limbless veterans in tattered uniforms begging on corners, the ragged street urchins who slept in doorways.

Had it been two dozen years since I was last here? Binh guided his Hyundai through the clot of zigzagging motorbikes and horn-tooting cars. For a disorienting moment, I felt like I was a 24-year-old sailor in scratchy new fatigues. I'd been plunged headlong into a living flashback: We were driving right down Bach Dang Avenue on the waterfront, and there—that four-story building right there had been my office. Hey, there was the statue of Tran Hung Dao in that little park I used to sit in over my lunch hour, just like I remembered it. There were the wide, leafy boulevards I remembered, lined with those colonial-era buildings sporting orangy terra-cotta roofs and wrought-iron doors and balconies, an architecture as thickset and straightforward as a French bourgeois.

Bounty of the fertile Mekong Delta, rice is harvested on a state farm near Can Tho, where farmers grow two and sometimes three crops a year. Rice helps fuel Vietnam's export economy and feeds a population that little more than a decade ago teetered on the brink of famine.

Traffic whirls along Le Loi Boulevard in front of the Rex Hotel, a French colonial landmark in downtown Saigon, now officially named Ho Chi Minh City. During the Vietnam War, the hotel was an American officers' barracks and scene of the daily—and contentious—military press briefings dubbed the "Five O'Clock Follies" by war correspondents.

The same exuberant street life I remembered from two decades before surged all around. Beneath the blight of billboards plastered to the sides of buildings—a roster of the world's leading electronics manufacturers—sidewalk vendors were still selling postcards and maps, colonial stamp and coin collections, French and American cigarettes. Matrons with shopping bags pattered down the street in baggy black trousers and conical hats. And strolling gracefully along were those delicate Saigon belles, their long hair gleaming black in the sunlight— looking younger and lovelier than ever in their flowery, flowing ao dai (or designer jeans).

It was all so uncanny. I recognized nearly everything. I was of course familiar with the layout of the city, which is rendered a virtual island by a circle of waterways—the Saigon River to the east, the tributary Thi Nghe River to the north, and a network of converging rivers and canals on the south and west. The city's most prominent landmark lies in District 1—Reunification Palace, known as Independence Palace before 1975, when it was the home of the president of South Vietnam. That '60s-mod white monolith provides a handy reference point in fixing city sights. Abutting the palace grounds on the southwest is shady Van Hoa Park. A few blocks beyond spreads the warren of Cholon, the Chinese quarter. Northeast of the palace, up tree-lined Le Duan Boulevard—a street pretty enough to rival any in Paris—loom the twin spires of the redbrick Notre Dame Cathedral. Farther along Le Duan, the green expanse of Saigon's Zoo and Botanical Gardens shoulders against a curve of the Thi Nghe River. Just southeast of the palace, concentrated in the several blocks running down to the Saigon River, are the city's best restaurants, shops, and hotels—the area through which we were now passing.

But something was wrong with this picture. I expected to find Saigon much as I'd left it—steamy, tattered, and vulgar, simultaneously repellent and fascinating, like a raunchy pulp novel you can't put down. I did see a few street kids and disabled vets

hanging about, hoping to put the touch on tourists, but where was the stream of in-your-face hookers, pickpockets, and other ne'er-do-wells that I recalled so vividly from before? Where were the sandbags and the concertina wire? Strangest of all, where was the *filth*, the layers of grime that had muted the buildings' pastel walls? This part of the city at least was clean—buffed to a high gloss, fountains fountaining, parks and gardens well-tended. The whole

Bound for jungles and rubber plantations of War Zone C northwest of Saigon, a tank of the U.S. 25th Infantry Division rolls through the South Vietnamese capital shortly after disembarking from a Navy ship in March 1966.

place seemed to have been given a fresh coat of paint. Maybe there was something to the old "Pearl of the Orient" tag after all.

We turned off Bach Dang Avenue (now called Ton Duc Thang Street) and headed up broad Nguyen Hue Boulevard, which blossoms during the Tet holiday with a curb-to-curb, brought-to-you-in-living-color flower market. At the opposite end of the street, another old acquaintance rose in a flurry of turrets and balustrades, columns and graceful arches—the sprawling two-story hunk of turn-of-the-century gingerbread known as the Hotel de Ville, city hall under the French. Today, the Ho Chi Minh City People's Committee was clicking around on the marble floors inside those elegant, chandelier-lit chambers. Outside, beneath the clock tower and classical

friezes, the red banner of Communist Vietnam stood out like a bloodstain against the yellow stucco.

I was staying just a few doors down from the old city hall, at the venerable Rex Hotel, a bachelor officers' quarter during the war and site of the famous "Five O'Clock Follies," in which a skeptical press was briefed on war developments by the Joint U.S. Public Affairs Office. The Rex commands one of the famous crossroads of Saigon, Nguyen Hue and Le Loi Boulevards. The tree-lined avenues converge at a circular fountain that may be the most photographed spot in the city. Approaching that intersection, we passed a pair of the glut of new-breed hotels springing up downtown. The Kimdo, operated by the state-run SaigonTourist, and the Century Saigon, a Hong Kong joint venture, are part of a trend toward ostentatiousness aimed at visiting businessmen on expense accounts. Overmarbled and overpriced, such Johnny-come-latelies can't match the ambience of older places like the Rex.

Who is staying in the new froufrou hotels—the ne-plus-ultra Omni and New World? Executives from Motorola and Citibank, France Telecom and Daewoo. Hanoi may be the place where investors go to seek permits, to try to cut through the red tape that binds Vietnam in shackles of kickbacks and special deals, but Saigon is where they come to *make money*. This boomtown is Vietnam's commercial engine, accounting for a third of the entire country's 24-billion-dollar-a-year economy. Entrepreneurship has never been a stranger here, and once the stifling policies of central planning began to wither away after 1986, the free market was quick to bounce back. Witness all the shops bulging with stereos, refrigerators, and TVs; the thicket of new skyscrapers cluttering the skyline; the factories going up on the outskirts of town—making everything from cosmetics to lubricants to window blinds.

Saigon now sports a modern shopping mall with a 32-lane bowling alley. The city even boasts the ultimate symbol of capitalism, a Mercedes-Benz showroom. You have to wonder who'll buy those

cars, though. It certainly won't be any of the un- or underemployed residents of Saigon's teeming slums—many of them people who were on the wrong side during the war, or disappointed farmers lured to the city by the prospect of an annual income three to four times the national average. "In Ho Chi Minh City, there are now two classes," Giang told me, "very rich and very poor. Saigon is a big trap. There's no self-control."

Self-control was never one of Saigon's virtues. The city has always been a nest of whores and thieves. I remember the black market frenzy of the war, when the sidewalks were lined with tables groaning under stacks of L&Ms and Tareytons, Gilbey's Gin and Johnnie Walker Red. Everyone was in on the take in one way or another. What started

with mama-sans peddling hot Timexes ran all the way up to President Nguyen Van Thieu and his larcenous cronies. There seemed to be something inherently corrupting about Saigon. Even now, after all the years they'd spent purging the "undesirable elements" of southern culture, the northern rulers of Vietnam almost seemed to have written off the south as decadent beyond salvation. Make money in Saigon and spend it in Hanoi—that was the best approach, Giang assured me.

Inside the Rex, I followed the white liveried bellhop up to my room. Though small, it carried the patina of authenticity, with a decor of rattan and varnished mahogany. I rode the elevator up to the rooftop restaurant, where I leaned against the waist-high railing and looked down at the traffic swirling

On their way to become stir-fried delicacies, live geese burden a motorbike in Cholon, the Chinese quarter of Saigon, where ethnic-Chinese entrepreneurs are helping to breathe new life into the Vietnamese economy.

around the fountain in front of the hotel. Strings of Hondas slid this way and that like beads on an abacus. Even from six stories up, the street noise was a high-voltage hum. What an adventure awaited me down there—crossing the street in Saigon! At intersections without stoplights you're forced to take a deep breath, step out into the crush of motorbikes—a million of 'em, it's said—and try to keep the faith that they'll part around you like ocean waters in a biblical miracle.

Stretching northwest from the fountain to the Hotel de Ville was a grassy, block-long park, whose most prominent feature had obviously been added since my day—a heroic statue of Ho Chi Minh. Back downstairs, I fended off the cadre of peddlers lurking outside the entrance to the Rex and crossed the street to Ho Chi Minh Park. Up close, I could see that Ho was protectively cradling a child. The statue was a popular site for photographs. While I stood there, a parade of Vietnamese families and couples posed in front of the gray stone effigy.

On across the park, I passed a towering sign proclaiming the Queen Bee dance hall. A smaller sign next door indicated the Eden shopping center. That building had housed offices of the international press and wire services during the war, above an arcade of shops that had once been the toniest in Vietnam. A walk through the arcade revealed that many of the shops were closed now. I thought of another Eden shopping center not far from my home—the bright, bustling mall in Arlington, Virginia, run by Vietnamese exiles. Had the owners of Saigon's Eden complex started over in a new land? That would have been a distinct possibility, but the reverse was becoming more commonplace in Saigon today. Growing numbers of *Viet Kieu*, overseas Vietnamese, are returning to their now more tolerant homeland, bringing with them capitalist skills and desperately needed infusions of cash.

I emerged from the dim Eden complex into the sunshine and the uproar of Le Loi Boulevard. This was the Saigon of old. Peddlers were carrying

Going vertical, the new Plaza Hotel reaches for the sky in Saigon, a bustling metropolis of some five million people and the largest city in Vietnam. Once called the Pearl of the Orient, Saigon retains the French colonial architecture and sidewalk cafés of an earlier day, though the central business district is becoming overshadowed by the flurry of new high rises being built (left).

beautifully carved model junks, some of them three or four feet long. Dangling from curbside racks were cleverly wrought toy aircraft—swept-wing F-4 Phantoms and Cobra helicopter gunships—all fashioned from flattened Coca-Cola or Tiger Beer cans. Kiosks and roving news hawkers sold copies of *USA Today* and the *International Herald-Tribune* (five dollars U.S. a pop). If you stopped to buy anything, or even to browse, toothless old women sprang genie-like right out of the sidewalk to tug at your sleeve and beg for a few dong.

A block-long promenade with trees and planters of flowers—Lam Son Square—ran down the center of Le Loi. To the south, the little park looked out over the fountain marking the intersection with Nguyen Hue Boulevard; to the north, it fronted Dong Khoi Street (Tu Do Street in my time, Rue Catinat to the French). Directly across that broad swath of asphalt stood a striking white building with a lofty, arching entryway, the Municipal Theatre. Built in 1899, the airy structure had been the wartime home of the South Vietnamese National Assembly. Once, a monumental statue of a South Vietnamese soldier had stood facing the National Assembly building. That figure was torn down in 1975, no doubt smashed to bits—filler for the road to the workers' paradise.

From the stone steps of the Municipal Theatre, the view was open all the way down Le Loi to the equestrian statue in the traffic roundabout fronting the Ben Thanh Market, the city's main retail marketplace, about five blocks to the south. The air hung thick and damp, tinged with blue from all the exhaust fumes. I peeked in the doors of the glass-fronted theater, now the site of nightly entertainments, everything from gymnastics to Vietnamese opera. The tables of an upscale new watering hole, the Q Bar, spilled out of the east side of the building into a little garden. A couple of Western swells sat sipping tall drinks.

On the west side of the plaza in front of the Municipal Theatre, sparkling once again with a fresh coat of paint, was the Continental, the gracious turn-of-the-century hotel that had figured in Graham Greene's 1955 novel *The Quiet American*. I was disappointed to see that the hotel's terrace bar, the storied Continental Shelf—a hangout for every journalist who passed through Saigon during both the French and American wars—was now closed in, reincarnated as Chez Guido, a fancy Italian eatery. I'd had some of the best gin and tonics of my life in that bar. On the opposite side of the plaza was another old-line Saigon hotel, the Caravelle, where Vietnam War-era journalists used to gather at night in the rooftop bar and watch the flares light up the paddies beyond the city like a Fourth of July display.

This whole area around Lam Son Square had been the epicenter of wartime Saigon's after-dark action. The four blocks of Tu Do Street that ran eastward from the square down to the waterfront had held more bars and witnessed more acts of indecency than any proper person would care to consider. In Vietnamese, "tu do" means "liberty," and the word took on a wide-ranging interpretation in those randy nightspots. Tu Do Street had been the Coney Island of Hell. Beckoning neon signs threw garish primary colors on the faces of the GIs, dope peddlers, and tough-talking tarts who swarmed the sidewalks in their fevered pursuits. I'd visited Tu Do not long after I arrived in-country and had been as shocked by the scene there as by any battlefield horror I had imagined.

What went on in those bars didn't originate with the arrival of the Americans. Under the French, the city was notorious for its opium dens, gambling clubs, and bordellos. The action missed a few beats after 1954, when Ngo Dinh Diem emerged as the new ruler in the southern, non-Communist half of the country. The puritanical Catholic Diem, along with his sleek and sinister sister-in-law, Madame Nhu—the heartless, edict-issuing Dragon Lady— took the spritz out of Saigon nightlife for a while. But with Diem's assassination in 1963, the trade in the city's fleshpots roared back with the resilience of

a gonococcal infection, and it would keep on roaring until the Communists closed things down in 1975.

So what was the action on Tu Do—Dong Khoi— today? I set off toward the waterfront to find out. During that four-block stroll, something happened that hadn't occurred during all the years of our involvement in Vietnam: An American male walked down that street without once being propositioned. At least not by any of those graphically lewd members

of the demimonde (I didn't count the oily money changer who attached himself to my arm for a short ways). I did get propositioned by a fellow eager to interest me in an expensive French fountain pen, and by a woman who thought that I simply couldn't return home without one of the hand-carved wooden sculptures she was selling. I was happy to discover that the dives of Tu Do Street have given way to the respectable shops of Dong Khoi—stores selling stationery and handicrafts, fine art and antiques. I spent several pleasant minutes browsing in an antiquarian bookshop, immersed in the mildewy smell that old tomes in the tropics take on.

At the end of the street I came to a Saigon landmark, the Majestic Hotel—the dowager queen of the waterfront, its outside as frilly as a lace doily.

Twisted wreckage of a car blown up by a Communist bomb lies on a cordoned-off Saigon street. Headquarters of the Military Assistance Command, Vietnam (MACV)—the overall U.S. command— Saigon was a frequent target of terrorism.

Black smoke towers over Saigon from fires touched off by Viet Cong attacks during the 1968 Tet Offensive. In the opening hours of the battle, Communist guerrillas breached the walls of the U.S. Embassy before they were killed by military policemen.

I turned north along the waterfront and its line of new floating restaurants. The sounds were those of a busy port city—the whistle of freighters arriving at the commercial docks just downriver, the drawl of diesel-powered cranes unloading cargo. After a long block, I came to Me Linh Square. Stone benches and planters of flowering bushes wrapped around the park's large, semicircular pool. A couple of kids were fishing with makeshift poles. I'd made many a lunch-hour

Young woman wears a face mask to help filter fumes on the choked streets of Saigon. Some city officials worry that rapid economic development will bring the same environmental ills that affect other booming Asian metropolises.

Rich and poor mingle on the sometimes mean streets of Saigon, where a beggar approaches a patron in an ice-cream parlor. Police sometimes sweep the downtown streets clear of the homeless and destitute. Some of those who have fallen through the socialist safety net had ties to the old South Vietnamese regime.

excursion to this park from my office at Vietnamese Naval Headquarters, half a block to the north. I used to sit and watch the ferry come and go, while dilapidated sampans putt-putted along like scruffy water bugs.

I took a seat now and craned my neck to view the dark, roughhewn statue of Tran Hung Dao, striding purposefully up there on his tall concrete pedestal. Decked out in 13th-century battle gear, the military hero rested his left hand on the hilt of his sword. His right arm was outstretched, pointing directly at the Saigon River. For a short time, a statue of the Trung Sisters—the revered leaders of Viet-nam's first rebellion against the Chinese, back in the first century—had presided over Me Linh Square. The monument was erected by President Diem's highly unpopular sister-in-law, Madame

Nhu, who had promoted the fantastic notion that she was the reincarnation of the heroic Trung Sisters. That explained why the statues bore a striking resemblance to Madame Nhu herself, a similarity that contributed to the sisters' brief reign over the Saigon waterfront. The two figures were pulled down after the Dragon Lady fled into exile following Diem's assassination.

North of the square, I stopped in a little river-

side plaza decorated with old ceremonial cannons. Across the street stood a four-story structure with green shutters and wide verandas wrapping around every floor. The building and those in the courtyard next to it had been the headquarters of the South Vietnamese Navy, a role indicated by the little blue anchor designs on the outside walls. I'd spent about half my tour in Vietnam in a dark, cool, fourth-floor office in that mustard yellow edifice.

I wondered if there was any way that I'd be allowed to revisit my old haunts. Probably not. It looked like the place was still being used by the military—there was an armed guard by the main gate. Suddenly thunder boomed across the river. I felt the ground vibrate beneath my feet, as if the cannons next to me had just gone off. Gray clouds were

Dusk settles over the Saigon River. The city languished after the collapse of the American-backed government in 1975, but today the wharves of the old French port are clogged with ships, as Saigon has reemerged as Vietnam's commercial center and magnet for foreign investment. Greeters in traditional dress welcome passengers from a luxury cruise ship.

Saigon models primp and powder their noses before a show of Vietnamese-made fashions in the French colonial-era Municipal Theatre, which once housed the South Vietnamese National Assembly.

rolling in, harbingers of the upcoming May-to-November rainy season, when afternoon thunderheads stack up above the city like thousand-story piles of dirty snowdrifts.

ALONE WITH THE PALACE GHOSTS

I'd driven past the old presidential palace too many times to count during the days when Nguyen Van Thieu was ensconced there, thanks to his political conniving and lukewarm American support. General Thieu had moved in after his election in 1967, and he didn't move out until April 21, 1975, when he realized the war was lost. Thieu fled to Taiwan with his family and a sizable chunk of ill-gotten gains; today the ex-president lives in England. Now I was going to get to bump around inside Thieu's old home.

I hopped out of my pedicab on Nguyen Du Street, at the eastern gate to the palace grounds. An asphalt lane led across a lawn just about large enough to accommodate the World Cup soccer finals. Together with the adjacent Van Hoa Park, this expanse of gardens, fountains, and towering trees constitutes one of the largest swatches of greenery in the city. From the street, the mammoth, modernistic palace looks like a sterile white box, but up close it's much more interesting. An elaborate decorative screen made up of rows of hourglass-shaped concrete spindles—designed as protection against incoming rockets—stretches across most of the facade. Much of the first floor is inset behind an open gallery with multiple pillars, creating the impression that the three remaining floors are floating above the ground.

Across the palace grounds, close to the main entrance off Nam Ky Khoi Nghia Street, sat a squatty green Russian T54 tank, Number 843 of the 2nd Army of North Vietnam. This was the tank that had crashed through the palace's curlicued iron gates on the morning of April 30, 1975. Tank 843 was commanded by an officer named Bui Quang Than. When he and his men reached the palace, they had only two rounds of ammunition left. "We shot twice," Than recalled later, "but it didn't work. So we had to break the gate down." It was Than who raced to the fourth floor of the palace and replaced the flag of South Vietnam with the Communist banner, signaling the reunification of his country after 21 years.

Today, Reunification Palace is preserved as a museum and occasionally used for receptions and government meetings. Inside the front entrance, I joined a group of Vietnamese visitors awaiting a tour. I was the only English-speaker, so I had to wait for a separate guide. Eventually a courtly Vietnamese beauty in a red ao dai arrived to escort me around the first floor. (I would have a sequence of guides, each assigned to a limited portion of the building.)

My guide gave me the basic introduction to the premises: four main floors plus a basement, 95 rooms in all. The initial impression of the building was one of openness, a feeling created by the high ceilings and cavernous rooms. In the first-floor cabinet room, I saw where Thieu and the military and civilian yes-men he surrounded himself with had sat around a long oval table. One of the criticisms leveled against the South Vietnamese leader was that he valued

To be rich is glorious: Millionaire Le Van Kiem limbers up before teeing off at a golf course outside Saigon. A Communist Party member sent south in 1976, Kiem made his fortune in the garment business and by building suburban homes from kits imported from the United States.

loyalty over ability—not surprising in a country of coups, plots, and counterplots. After the departure of the Americans, Thieu's battle-shunning generals failed him again and again.

In the palace's basement—a bomb-proof warren of narrow passageways and claustrophobic window-less rooms—the president had received news of those failures. In the combat command center, wall maps showed the troop strengths of allied forces deployed

A setting in Graham Greene's novel The Quiet American, *the turn-of-the-century Continental Hotel presides over downtown Saigon's Dong Khoi Street. During the Vietnam War, spies and war correspondents gathered on the hotel's veranda, the storied Continental Shelf. Doormen greet visitors at the Majestic Hotel, another recently renovated Saigon landmark.*

around South Vietnam. Situation maps showed Communist bases, and one map recorded the length of the Ho Chi Minh Trail. In a telex room, I saw the humpy old machines that had once clattered with the incoming news of the fall of Danang. Spartan gray and green metal radio equipment, labeled with their American manufacturer and points of origin—GE, Chicago, New York—filled the communications center. Thieu had broadcast to his people over these machines, trying to put his own spin on events that were spinning out of his control. I could almost feel the panic that must have filled these subterranean chambers as word came in that the South's defenses were crumbling.

Up on the second floor, my guide led the way to a cavernous, red-carpeted conference hall. It was here

Downtown Saigon hot spot, the Lemon Grass Restaurant serves artfully presented portions of Vietnam's world-famous cuisine. Vietnamese food, which reflects French and Chinese influence, may be some of the healthiest in all of Asia with its liberal amounts of fresh vegetables and lean meats, cooked in just a touch of oil.

that Gen. Duong Van Minh—"Big Minh" as he was called—the man who replaced Thieu during those last desperate days of the Republic of Vietnam, officially surrendered to Lt. Col. Bui Van Tung, the ranking North Vietnamese officer on the scene when the palace was overrun. "I have been waiting since early this morning to transfer power to you," General Minh said as Tung entered the conference hall. "There is no question of your transferring power," Tung replied. "You cannot give up what you do not have."

The second floor contained the most beautiful rooms in the palace. In the National Reception Room, a formal chamber with ivory-upholstered chairs and an ornate Oriental rug, the president symbolically sat on the same level with his countrymen; in the International Reception Room, however—a

chamber ablaze with red carpeting and red brocaded chairs—Thieu sat on a dais above his guests, a bit of chauvinist symbolism that had to rankle his American benefactors.

Nearby, the Credentials Presenting Room represented the zenith of Vietnamese decorative arts, with enough gilt to send the needle of a giltometer right off the dial: a lacquerware desk, coffee tables, and chairs glinting with gold-embellished rosettes; a wall-size lacquerware painting depicting the 2,000-year sweep of Vietnamese history in splashes of crimson, green, and gold; several tall golden vases echoing the fluted design of the palace's facade. The regal, airy hallway just outside the chamber was graced with one of the most beautiful Oriental rugs I've ever seen, an immense circular creation on which golden dragons writhed on a bright red background.

My third-floor hostess escorted me to the president's private office and library, a wood-paneled room that Ward Cleaver might have felt at home in. There was a private movie theater with red plush seats, and a gambling room with a bar and tables set up for mah-jongg. It was off this floor, in back of the palace, that Thieu had ushered his fleeing family aboard a helicopter on a terrace landing pad. That helicopter is still there, looking sad and abandoned.

Here on the third floor, my guide showed me into a small, spartan room that serves a purpose different from in the days of President Thieu. The room was equipped with a television and video player. The guide indicated that I should sit down. I did as I was instructed while the woman inserted a tape in the VCR. She flipped off the light and stepped outside, closing the door behind her. I was the only person in the room. I felt like a patient undergoing an MRI.

For the next 25 minutes I watched an encapsulated version of 30 years of Vietnamese history, from Ho Chi Minh's 1945 Declaration of Independence to the Liberation of Saigon. This was the winner's version of history, of course, but I found those grainy, flickering, black-and-white images compelling nonetheless. There were scenes of cocky, laughing French generals juxtaposed with Viet Minh soldiers hauling artillery up steep hillsides by hand for the final, climactic battle at Dien Bien Phu. Next came ghostly images of despondent French soldiers departing Vietnam for good in 1954. The video traced the rise of Diem in the South, the beginnings of civil war, and America's creeping involvement. I relived the shocking 1963 self-immolation of the monk Thich Quang Duc on a busy Saigon street. Even more shocking was the footage of Madame Nhu after a string of subsequent self-immolations: "Let them burn," she cackled, mockingly calling the suicides a "barbecue." She even belittled the monks for using imported petrol. Other footage showed the beautiful and imperious Madame Nhu as she stepped into her Rolls Royce, and as she spoke to the American press—

wearing dark glasses, no less! Here was a woman who tried to pass herself off as a Vietnamese heroine, yet who couldn't write a word in Vietnamese.

The scenes of the American phase of the war sped by in a familiar blur—Khe Sanh and the Tet Offensive of 1968, the bombing of North Vietnam, antiwar protests in the United States, the winding down of the American presence, and finally the quick series of North Vietnamese successes in 1975

that spelled the end of the three-decade-long conflict, symbolized by the helicopter evacuations from the roof of the U.S. Embassy and Communist tanks rolling down the streets of Saigon. Those were powerful images for an American to revisit. When the videotape ended, the national anthem of the Socialist Republic of Vietnam blared out at me, sitting alone in that darkened room. I felt weak in the knees.

I escaped out into the hallway before the music ended, looking for my guide. Surprisingly, no one was around. I even called out, but no one appeared. It was late in the day. Had everyone gone home? I still had the fourth floor to see, so I proceeded upstairs by myself. I came out on an open rooftop—only the central portion of the top floor is enclosed. I had a bird's-eye view of the tennis courts in back of the palace. There was little to see inside the enclosed area, only an empty "dance hall." Had Thieu and his cronies done the twist in there? The view from the open area was more interesting, a panorama of tree-tops and orange tile roofs in every direction.

The front of the building presented the prettiest view of Saigon I'd ever enjoyed—the wide prospect of Le Duan Boulevard, framed by parks on both sides, leading past the gray-slate spires of the Notre

In a dress of white lace, a Saigon bride receives a final touch-up before exchanging Roman Catholic vows in Notre Dame Cathedral. The century-old church in the heart of Saigon is the spiritual center of Vietnamese Catholicism, which still claims some six million adherents.

Dame Cathedral, string-straight all the way to the Zoo and Botanical Gardens. Here was one thing those colonialists had gotten right. When the French arrived in 1859, Saigon had been hardly more than a trading post, but over the next century the new masters of Saigon had built themselves a petit slice of home, a habitation of leafy boulevards and green parks, comfortable villas and fine public buildings— the Pearl of the Orient indeed. Now it all belonged to the Vietnamese.

I started back downstairs, still encountering no one. When I reached the first floor, I walked through the grand, empty corridors, beneath crystal chandeliers high overhead, my steps echoing on the glistening tile floors. For a moment, the ghosts of Vietnam's turbulent past seemed my only companions.

SULTRY NIGHTS IN OLD SAIGON

In the Rex's rooftop restaurant, I settled into a chair and watched the Saigon dusk merge into evening. The hoot of a ship's horn called softly from down on the river, a vessel headed for the delta and the sea and who knew where beyond? I felt a wave of nostalgia, an affection for this city that I'd never expected to feel. And I was beginning to succumb to a familiar temptress—the Saigon night, soft and voluptuous, enveloping in its warmth, full of the promise of pleasure, like the first sip of the gin and tonic the waiter had just set before me.

Across Ho Chi Minh Park were the first stirrings of this evening's festivities: A cluster of mini-skirted girls preened and posed outside the Queen Bee, waiting to snare escorts to the dance hall. In my hotel room I'd found an invitation to the Rex's own dance hall, with an admonition on the back: "Please don't accompany children under 16 years of age."

Down at the end of Ho Chi Minh Park, the Hotel de Ville was lit up like a yellow-frosted wedding cake. A circle of red lights flashed around the face of the clock on the central tower. It was after eight. Time to hit the streets. I descended into the maelstrom of light and motion, the pedestrians and peddlers, the motorbikes swirling around the fountain on Le Loi. With the darkness hiding any signs of scruffiness, downtown Saigon was stunning.

Heading for the waterfront, I grabbed a taxi— one of the burgeoning fleet of new Japanese imports that have replaced the old cream-and-blue Renaults of the war era. I happened to mention to the driver how much cleaner the city looked now than when I was here before. "Oh yes. Everything fixed up," the driver verified. "Security much better, too." Problems with thievery in Saigon are well documented. There are the crowds of playful kids who surround tourists and lift their valuables with the dexterity of the Artful Dodger, and also thieves who operate from motorbikes, grabbing purses or cameras from the shoulders of pedestrians. Down on the waterfront, roving transvestites pose as prostitutes, relieving

gullible male tourists of their watches or billfolds.

The city's seamier side reveals itself in other ways. Dope peddlers lurk outside popular downtown bars like Apocalypse Now, where American kids too young to remember the war like to gather for a watered-down rendition of illicit Saigon. And you'd have to be blind not to notice that prostitution is flourishing again, even if it is a long way from the old open raunchiness. Sometime during the course of nearly every pedicab ride I took—after the polite chatter about where I was from and the offer to wait for me to take me to my next destination—there came this question: "You want Vietnamese girl?"

I was even solicited right beside the Virgin Mary. During a walk, I'd stopped to rest on one of the park benches in the open, pleasant square in front of Notre Dame Cathedral, where a life-size Mary in white stone stands in a green plot ringed by low bushes and pots of red flowers. As I sat contemplating the Blessed Virgin's serene, alabaster-pure smile, a street character slid onto the bench beside me. His conversation began innocently enough, but when he mistakenly thought that I was ogling a young Vietnamese woman sitting on a bench behind the statue of Mary, he got down to cases: "You like?" he asked, jutting his chin toward the young woman and grinning suggestively. "Lot of pretty girls in Saigon, eh?" His voice became confidential. "I get you *three*-girl massage," he said, holding up three fingers to emphasize his point. "All very young. Very cheap."

You soon discover that in Saigon, innocent conversations are as rare as Huguenots.

Before chanting Buddhist monks at the Vinh Nghiem Pagoda, Saigon businesswoman Tran Thi Tuyet Mai and bridegroom Song Vudh Panranatakorn of Bangkok, Thailand, have their hours-old wedding vows sanctified. Traditional Vietnamese marriage ceremonies take place in the bride's home.

Saigon's licentious character seems endemic. That old, innocuous description of the shape of Vietnam—two rice baskets suspended at opposite ends of a long pole—really ought to give way to the image of a rampant dragon, its flared head in the north and its belly and tail in the south. That would place the brains and fangs and sexual organs all in their proper positions.

My taxi driver let me out on the waterfront at the foot of Nguyen Hue Boulevard. Across the river, the shoreline flashed with incandescent signs of commerce, paeans to Philips, Gold Star, Ricoh, Fuji, Heineken, DHL. On this side of the river, strung along Ton Duc Thang Street north toward Me Linh Square, the colored lights of floating restaurants pulsed like a mini-Las Vegas. Periodically, one of the restaurants would haul away from shore to chug up and down the river, shimmering against the black water like an abstract design on a lacquerware panel. Water taxis slid across the river from the opposite shore, their silhouettes scattering the colored reflections of the larger boats. Downriver, the liners that had put in for the night shone like floating cities.

The gangplank entryways of the restaurants rested on a narrow dock, and a tout was stationed at the foot of each gangplank, extolling the virtues of his establishment. As I strolled down the line of restaurants, dueling bands amped out a medley of '60s and '70s hits. I stopped in wonderment at the Ben Nghe Restaurant, which was shaped like a giant shark. Several patrons sat inside the gaping mouth of the creature, whose jagged teeth were outlined with lights. The band aboard this electrified man-eater was churning out a high-volume, dead-on rendition of "Black Magic Woman."

PAGODAS AND PACHYDERMS

Before being absorbed by Saigon, the district of Cholon, southwest of downtown, was a separate city inhabited by ethnic-Chinese. Traditionally the country's wealthiest citizens (they controlled nearly half of South Vietnam's economy), ethnic-Chinese were persecuted as "bourgeois elements" after 1975, causing a third of the population to flee to China and prompting that country's 1979 attack on Vietnam. I remembered Cholon as the most crowded part of the city, a maze of restaurants and small shops—with more pagodas than you could shake a joss stick at. Today, some of the entrepreneurs who fled during the late '70s are returning, bringing with them the financial skills that made Cholon a commercial dynamo (the name means "Big Market").

From the Rex, Giang and I took a taxi south along Tran Hung Dao Boulevard toward the Chinese quarter. The hotels and stores became progressively smaller and scruffier along the way. We got out at the Tam Son Hoi Quan Pagoda in the center of Cholon. Built in the 19th century by the Fujian congregation, the pagoda is dedicated to Me Sanh, the goddess of fertility. Locals come here to pray for children.

It was near here that President Diem and his brother met their end. The repressive Diem was widely hated—he alienated the peasants, persecuted the Buddhists and indigenous religious sects, toppled the influential Binh Xuyen crime syndicate, eliminated real and imagined Communists. Two of his own Air Force pilots had even tried to kill him by bombing the palace.

During a coup in November 1963, Diem and his brother had sought refuge in the Cha Tam Catholic Church a few blocks on down Tran Hung Dao Boulevard. They made the mistake of surrendering to the coup leaders, who sent an armored personnel carrier to pick them up. On the way back to Saigon, soldiers shot and stabbed the brothers to death. The news of their deaths set off public rejoicing. Political prisoners were freed from jail, and bars and nightclubs threw open their doors once more. (Just three weeks later, President Kennedy was assassinated. Since the Kennedy Administration had sanctioned the coup against Diem, some conspiracy theorists have linked Diem's family with Kennedy's death, as unlikely as that may seem.)

Giang and I walked in the direction of Cha Tam

Church. Our destination wasn't the church, but rather the Binh Tay Market, Cholon's main marketplace. On the way, we threaded cluttered, dirty side streets packed with humanity—people fixing flat tires, giving manicures, cutting hair, welding, pounding, sawing, standing around, scratching. There were closet-size restaurants from which the pungent odor of curry wafted forth. One depressing shop was selling mounted animal specimens and animal skins.

In contrast to the grittier parts of Cholon, the Binh Tay Market, a long, low-slung beige building with a pagoda-like clock tower and tile roof, was clean and thoroughly modern. By the main entrance, men pushed handcarts laden with bales of cloth goods. Arriving pedicabs were piled high with cases of soap powder. Motorbikes teetered up with crates of sardines strapped on the back. Lambrettas disgorged cartons of Nestle's Milo.

"This is where other markets in Vietnam get their supplies," Giang said, explaining that Binh Tay was a wholesale operation. "This is the biggest market in the country."

From here, the items would spread throughout the length of Vietnam. In Cholon, you can have your pick of pagodas and restaurants, but this was the real

Abandoned, misshapen children live at Saigon's Tu Du Hospital, a research center studying the long-term effects of dioxin—the active ingredient in Agent Orange. The chemical defoliant was sprayed by U.S. warplanes (above) across South Vietnam to deny hiding places to Communist forces. Vietnamese scientists claim as many as 500,000 children may have been born with dioxin-related deformities since the mid-1960s.

appeal of the Chinese quarter—the colorful hum and bustle of business.

To escape the rising heat, I abandoned Cholon's sun-scorched streets for the cool depths of Notre Dame Cathedral. A product of the 1880s, this old neo-Romanesque structure remains the spiritual center of Vietnamese Catholicism, which still claims some six million followers, even though until 1990 churches faced severe limitations on their activities. That was when the government began allowing a measure of religious freedom, with the stipulation that churches not undermine state authority. (Arrests continue for perceived public agitation by religious leaders.)

Bells were pealing out the call to noon mass. Inside the cathedral, a priest stood beneath a statue of Mary, speaking over a loudspeaker system to a smattering of parishioners, mostly women and old men. It was an electrifying—or, to be precise—*electrified* sight. Mary's halo was a circle of neon tubing, and below her, "Ave Maria" was spelled out in blue neon.

A short pedicab ride down Le Duan Boulevard from the cathedral is the Zoo and Botanical Gardens, which I'd visited on Sunday afternoons during the war. Returning now, I stepped through the iron gates onto a wide avenue lined with flower beds and stately, soaring trees, their trunks six feet or more in diameter. All the way down at the end of the road, an amusement park with antique carnival rides backed up against the Thi Nghe River. Groundskeepers puttered about in well-tended formal gardens on either side of the roadway. The zoo occupied a large tract to my right, mostly hidden among the trees. People lazed about on the open expanses of grass or sat on the gray stone benches lining the winding pathways.

To the immediate left was a rambling yellow stucco building with a pagoda-style tower—the city's History Museum, formerly the National Museum of the Republic of Vietnam. Built by the French in 1929, the exhibition hall guards a cache of artifacts tracing the cultures of Vietnam, from the Stone Age up to the present. Most fascinating was the display of pottery, baskets, and colorful clothing belonging to a sampling

Vietnamese nun prays on Palm Sunday in Cholon's Cha Tam Catholic Church. Foraging for his daily bowl of rice, a Buddhist monk begs for food or contributions of money on Ton That Dam Street in Saigon. Buddhism is Vietnam's dominant faith, with more than 4,700 active pagodas, although Confucianism, Taoism, and ancestor-worship play major roles in the lives of Vietnamese.

Betting on the ponies is frenzied most weekends at the Saigon Racetrack, which was built by the French at the turn of the century and reopened in 1989 after a 14-year hiatus under Communist rule. At an old Saigon health club, young men pump iron. The sports-conscious city hosts, among other events, a semiannual international marathon.

of Vietnam's ethnic minorities. It was hard to believe that such a small country could encompass the range of cultures represented by those everyday items.

Approaching the zoo, I wandered down a winding pathway to a little lake with an island bandstand. Huge green lily pads with pink and white flowers spread across the water. Beyond the lake, the zoo's animal cages spread out under the canopy of trees. I made a slow circuit, pausing to watch a sleek black panther pacing endlessly, and an Indian elephant displayed right out in the open, tethered by one foot. Chattering youngsters raced ahead of their parents from cage to cage. Lovers nestled together on benches. It occurred to me that if someone wanted to watch the people of Saigon just being themselves, they couldn't find a better place.

Day-Trippin' with the Viet Cong

My time was growing short, so I set about planning a daylong excursion to some of Saigon's outlying attractions. South of the city were the verdant rice fields and labyrinthine waterways of the Mekong Delta. But I'd already been in that direction back when I was stationed here, driving across the tabletop-flat landscape in an open jeep, immersed in the wet, earthy smell of the paddies. Just below the old southern capital, the Dong Nai River gathers the waters of the Saigon River on a looping path to the South China Sea, passing through the once Viet Cong–haunted Rung Sat Swamp along the way. Thinking of that broad brown waterway brought back memories—of still, sweltering days broken by the distant cries of fishing birds, of rice-laden

sampans and slow-moving junks, and the guttural thrumming of diesels driving cargo ships upriver to the docks of Saigon.

On this trip, I decided to range north of Saigon, to visit the famous Viet Cong tunnels in the rural district of Cu Chi. The museum and exhibits there tell the story of the underground Communist stronghold that had once spread from the Cambodian border right up to the outskirts of the South Vietnamese capital. Cu Chi had been part of the Communist-dominated Iron Triangle, some 125 square miles of territory bounded by the cities of Tay Ninh, Song Be, and Saigon. The tunnels honeycombing that region had allowed the Viet Cong to come and go like spirits, appearing from nowhere to strike without warning then vanishing into the earth.

Started in the 1940s during the insurgency against the French and expanded during the Vietnam War, the tunnel system included command posts, living areas, field hospitals, kitchens, weapons factories, and storage rooms, all knitted together by a spiderweb of passageways totaling some 150 miles in length. The Viet Cong had held out in this subterranean township against repeated sweeps by U.S. and South Vietnamese troops—though at a fearful toll. It was from the tunnels that VC guerrillas infiltrated Saigon during the Tet Offensive of 1968.

These days, it was often tubby Americans—or Taiwanese or Japanese—who were disappearing into the tunnels of Cu Chi. The place has become wildly popular with tourists. About an hour and a half after leaving Saigon, we were finally closing in on the tunnels. I looked out at a landscape of small rice plots, scrubby trees, and random clumps of grass. Once this had been fertile farmland and forests, before search-and-destroy missions wiped away whole villages, and the land was denuded with chemicals, fire, bombs, and enormous land-clearing plows.

Binh pulled off the road in front of the Cu Chi Tunnels museum, where the history of Cu Chi is related through a few simple displays and a brief

Symbol of a vanquished nation, Saigon's former Independence Palace—renamed Reunification Palace after the defeat of South Vietnam—sits at the end of tree-lined Le Duan Boulevard (opposite). Conquering North Vietnamese tanks smashed through the wrought-iron gates of the palace on April 30, 1975. Today the Communist Party uses the palace on ceremonial occasions, while its military command bunkers, helicopter landing pad, and lavish reception rooms are a major tourist attraction.

video. The young museum guide wore the black pajamas associated with the Viet Cong. She took her role quite seriously, never once smiling as she showed me hand axes and baskets used in the excavations, punji stakes placed in traps in and around the tunnels, a metal bomb fragment. Her tone was lecturing, reproving. These are things you need to be shown, her voice seemed to say. Once, when I started to ask her a question, she cut me off: "Keep calm."

I sat down to listen as the young woman talked about the layout of the tunnels, pointing to a map with lines radiating hither and yon. "Here at Dong Du, the 25th Infantry Division built a base camp above the tunnels." The young woman moved to a diorama showing a cutaway of a section of tunnels. The first level, about ten feet down, was where the

inhabitants slept and ate; a second level, 20 feet down, and a third, another ten feet lower, were connecting thoroughfares. Kerosene lamps were used for illumination, the woman explained, and a few tunnels even had electric lights. "Gen. William Westmoreland had this display constructed," she claimed.

A video followed the woman's talk. The first portion showed Cu Chi before 1967, when the district was thick with jungle and rubber plantations. Contented villagers grew vegetables and flowers. Those bucolic images were followed by battle scenes—first American warplanes, then farmers, women, and schoolgirls, all scurrying about with their weapons, firing at the sky and popping into tiny holes in the ground. Other scenes depicted the tunnel-dwellers taking apart unexploded bombs to make antipersonnel mines. It was a grim existence those people led. It's estimated that of 16,000 VC who served in the tunnels, only 6,000 survived. Much of the tunnel complex was finally destroyed when B-52s carpet-bombed the region in the late 1960s. By then, however, the course of the war had been set.

From the museum, Giang and I followed a Vietnamese soldier across the road (the facility is run by the military). A winding path led through a sun-dappled grove of eucalyptus trees interspersed with grasses and stands of wispy bamboo. Somewhere beneath our feet was the most interesting part of the exhibits, a section of the actual tunnels. We passed a crater from one of the bombs dropped by those B-52s. The hole was over 15 feet deep, as big around as a small house. The rusting hulk of an American M-41 tank destroyed by a land mine sat close by.

My guide paused beside a clump of grass that was cordoned off. The soldier leaned inside the ropes and pushed down on the corner of a trapdoor hidden by the grass. The door pivoted to reveal a ten-foot-deep hole roughly three by seven feet in dimension. Nasty-looking bamboo stakes, their tips sharpened to spearpoints, lined the bottom of the pit.

"Stakes poisoned with cobra venom," the guide announced, chuckling at the cleverness of the trap.

Farther on, the guide squatted beside a small bush. He reached into the center of the plant and—presto—jerked it out of the ground. The bush had disguised an astoundingly small tunnel opening—little bigger than a shoe box. The soldier slipped into the opening feet first and pulled the lid back into place as he disappeared. The entrance was invisible.

A few moments later the guide reemerged. "Every day, American soldier up here," he said, "Cu Chi people down there."

The openings were positioned every 50 yards or so, and their doors had frequently been rigged with mines. The size of the tunnels—about a foot and a half wide and two feet high—prevented most Americans from entering (as if anyone in his right mind would want to), although specially trained "tunnel rats" descended into those confining passages to ferret out the VC.

For bulky Westerners interested in sampling the tunnels, a section has been enlarged to twice the original dimensions. Giang and I followed the guide into the mouth of this tourist tunnel. The hard, dry subsoil of the ceiling and walls was the texture and color of concrete, which explained why there was no need to reinforce the excavations. The guide's flashlight revealed the tunnel stretching away into dim uncertainty, like a view of a lower intestine. The soldier motioned for us to follow and scurried ahead. There must have been something in his genes, for Giang took to this right away, following close behind the guide. After duck-walking a few feet down the passageway, I stopped short. It was spooky down there, hot and still. The tunnel ahead looked like nothing more than a drainpipe. That's when my latent claustrophobia kicked in—and I had to get out, fast.

I scooted out of that burrow backwards like I'd been poked with a cattle prod, not stopping till I was safely outside in the sunlight. I sat on the edge of the entrance for a minute just gulping air, glad to be clear of that hellhole. What a nightmare it must have

been to be inside there when the bombs were raining down. After seeing this place, I had to salute the tenacity of the Viet Cong.

I asked later how the people of Cu Chi had known where they were inside the maze of passages.

"Habit," our guide said, "like you learn the way around your city."

We ended the tour in an underground kitchen. Another Vietnamese soldier was tending a large blackened pot on a wood-burning stove. The soldier motioned for Giang and me to sit, then he fetched chunks of a pale vegetable from the pot and gave one to each of us to sample. I took a tentative bite. The two soldiers watched with anticipation, smiling broadly when I showed a favorable reaction. The vegetable was soft and mealy, like a potato that had been overcooked.

"What is it?" I asked.

"Cassava. A staple of the Viet Cong. They cultivated it hidden among clumps of grasses and harvested it at night."

What an unbelievable experience, to be sharing the food of the former enemy, in this setting that had witnessed so much fighting and dying—on both sides. It seemed a miracle that we were able to talk about it now.

I skipped the immensely popular firing range at Cu Chi, where for a dollar a cartridge, visitors can deplete their savings with an AK-47. (Flush Japanese tourists, restricted from access to guns back home, have been known to fire off a hundred-dollar burst with glee.) I browsed for a short time in the souvenir shop that everyone is shepherded through on exiting the tour. There was an interesting collection of cigarette lighters made from old mortar casings, and you could take home a VC-style floppy green jungle hat or black-and-white check neck scarf. But I already had my souvenir from Cu Chi—the image of the smiling faces of those Vietnamese soldiers as I'd sampled their food.

Another hour and a half to the northwest, just this side of the Cambodian border, I was the one doing the smiling, at the sight of one of the most original structures in the world of religion, the Cao Dai Great Temple of Tay Ninh. My smiles were those of wonder—for this building, and the religion it represents, are nothing short of amazing. A sort of spiritual slumgullion, the Cao Dai doctrine tosses together healthy portions of Buddhism, Confucianism, and Taoism, then adds a handful of Hinduism, a pinch of Islam, a dollop of Christianity, and a sprinkling of Vietnamese ancestor-worship. Founded in Tay Ninh Province in 1926 by civil servant and mystic Ngo Minh Chieu, the Cao Dai sect claims to receive its divine truths directly from the spirit world via seances, reportedly communicating at times with the likes of Joan of Arc, William Shakespeare, Victor Hugo, René Descartes, and Vladimir Ilyich Lenin.

Only a year after its founding, this wildly eclectic faith claimed some 26,000 followers, and by the mid-1950s, the religion had spread throughout southern Vietnam. In Tay Ninh Province, the Cao Dai ran their own feudal state, with a private army. The army was absorbed into the forces of the South in 1956, and throughout the Vietnam War, the Cao Dai refused to support the Viet Cong. As a result, the Cao Dai were persecuted after the war. Their lands were confiscated, and four adherents were executed in 1979. In 1985, however, the Cao Dai temples were returned. Today some three million Vietnamese ascribe to the faith, concentrated in Tay Ninh Province and the Mekong Delta.

For such a colorful religion, no drab, understated house of worship would do. The Cao Dai Great Temple, constructed between 1933 and 1955, resembles something that might have sprung from an opium dream. I arrived at the temple during a memorial service and was allowed to observe from the second-story balcony. A series of paired columns marched away toward the front of the sanctuary, each column entwined with bright merry-go-round figures—glazed ceramic dragons with gaping duck-like bills, scaly serpentine bodies, and red-and-white candy-cane horns. The pale blue domed ceiling, with

American GI dog tags, for sale to tourists on the streets of Saigon, along with wartime memorabilia from gas masks to flak jackets, serve as reminders that some of the war's deadliest killing fields bordered the South Vietnamese capital. South of Saigon, GIs of the 9th Infantry Division slog through the muck (opposite).

Former enemies meet at Cu Chi, a rural district northwest of Saigon that was part of the Iron Triangle, a Viet Cong-dominated region veined with some 150 miles of tunnels. At today's popular Cu Chi museum, a soldier shows a hidden entrance to the subterranean network, which included living quarters, kitchens, and hospitals. For a dollar a bullet, tourists, including this American war veteran, can fire M-16 or AK-47 rifles.

its dozens of mirror-finish stars, seemed to have been modeled on the Hayden Planetarium. Tall stained-glass windows lined both sides of the long, narrow chamber. In the center of each was the supreme symbol of the Cao Dai, the all-seeing "One Eye of God," peering out from a golden triangle (and looking remarkably like the figure on the back of a dollar bill).

The members of the congregation, some 200 or more strong—women to the left, men to the right—knelt on the tile floor, each person robed in white. White headbands distinguished the family members of the deceased. A half-dozen Cao Dai priests, garbed in red, blue, or yellow robes, stood at an altar midway down the chamber. Everyone was repeating a sing-song chant. Over and over they droned the words in unison. The sound began to have a hypnotic effect.

Giang had waited for me outside the temple. As I stood looking up at the One Eye of God over the front door, at the multitiered Oriental roof capped with towers and domes and embellished with human and animal figures, he said quite simply: "I don't understand this religion. It is...extra-ordinary."

A Case of Namstalgia

My last afternoon in Vietnam had finally come. I decided to spend it just goofing off, and the pool at the Rex seemed a fine place for it. As the afternoon wore on, I shook myself from my poolside lethargy. A gin and tonic down at the Givral Café was on my mind. That hospitable old establishment occupies a corner on Lam Son Square just a few doors down from the Continental Hotel and directly opposite the Municipal Theatre. Always a good spot for keeping an eye on downtown doings, the café had been one of the chief rumor mills during the war.

Gray thunderheads were gathering over Lam Son Square when I ducked into the Givral at four o'clock. I took a seat at a small table covered with a white linen cloth. Just outside, newspaper hawkers held the afternoon editions up to the window, trying to catch my eye. Moments later, fat raindrops were bubbling on Dong Khoi Street. Steam rose like a

layer of ground fog from the hot black asphalt. The warm air, tinged with the smell of ozone, was so thick you could almost drink it. Geckos darted across the walls of the café. I sipped my gin and watched the day darken dramatically, the sun eclipsed by the tropical downpour. A pair of teenage beauties rode past on a motorbike, drenched to the skin, laughing, their teeth a luminous white.

In ten minutes, the shower was over. Shafts of sunlight pierced the parting clouds, illuminating the wet leaves of the trees along Le Loi. Suddenly I was thinking of other evenings in another time, when I had sat just like this, watching the flow of traffic after a rain. Old images drifted up from subconscious depths: Visions of young women with perfect posture riding their bicycles majestically past my

sidewalk refuge. A bare electric bulb burning orange-yellow down a narrow alley across the way. Doll-like children resuming their games of badminton. Old men shuffling along, their sandals slapping sidewalks covered with tiny blossoms washed down from the tamarind trees. Surely this was the hour of nostalgia for anyone who'd ever experienced Saigon.

I was still feeling nostalgic that night, looking down from the roof of the Rex at the traffic inching around the fountain on Le Loi. The Sunday evening ritual of *song tu do* ("living free") was in full swing—a tire-to-tire, high-decibel mass frenzy in which the city's upper-class youth, all dressed up with no place to go, endlessly cruise the downtown intersections on their motorbikes. The traffic crept up one side of Ho Chi Minh Park and down the other, packed together

Farmer near Tay Ninh tends his paddies beneath the cloud-wreathed peak known to American soldiers and airmen as Black Virgin Mountain. The mountain was within the Iron Triangle, a 125-square-mile territory bounded by the cities of Tay Ninh, Song Be, and Saigon. Air assaults throughout this region included frequent use of napalm. An Air Force A-1 Skyraider (opposite) drops its payload on a Viet Cong position.

Preceding pages: Worshippers lay prostrate in prayer at the Cao Dai Great Temple near Tay Ninh. Cao Dai doctrine fuses elements of Buddhism, Confucianism, Taoism, Hinduism, Islam, and Christianity. Founded by a Vietnamese mystic in 1926, the colorful religion today claims some three million followers, mostly in Tay Ninh Province and the Mekong Delta.

Lay priest summons the faithful to prayers at the Cao Dai Great Temple, one of the world's most striking houses of worship. The "One Eye of God" is the supreme symbol of the Cao Dai faith, which claims to receive divine guidance via seances, reportedly communicating with such diverse spirits as Joan of Arc, René Descartes, William Shakespeare, Louis Pasteur, and Vladimir Lenin.

like microbes in a petri dish. I had no intention of venturing out of the hotel. I would have had to walk on the shoulders of those kids to cross the street.

I wondered what people were doing up in Hanoi this night. I knew that some of them at least were enjoying a concert of songs by the famous South Vietnamese composer Trinh Cong Son. His works were written during the war, in the 1950s and '60s. "All his songs were performed by the love of his life, Miss Khanh Ly," Giang had told me. "Their story is like Romeo and Juliet—eternal love." Those old love songs and antiwar songs were packing them in. According to the papers, the concert had sold out two days in advance. Scalpers were commanding three times the face value for tickets. What was it about those songs that touched the people of the north? The headline about the concert in *Vietnam News* read: "Nostalgic night a Hanoi sellout."

Nostalgia...Namstalgia. We were all susceptible to it in varying degrees, and for far different reasons. For the Vietnamese, it must have sprung from reminiscences about the hour of their victory, so long and costly in the attainment. Yes, the country had been made politically whole in 1975, but even today there are gulfs remaining to be bridged. The government of Vietnam has seemed more open to reconciliation with America than with some of its own people, such as the soldiers who died for the South, whose graves have been desecrated, bulldozed under, forgotten. Or the former southern soldiers who are buried alive by their jobless status. Much remains to be done to insure that the north and the south are truly united. Perhaps that victory will have to wait for the next generation to achieve.

On my final morning in Saigon, I paid a visit to the War Relics Museum, housed in the former home of the U.S. Information Service, just north of Reunification Palace. I wanted to see for myself what the Vietnamese have chosen to say about the war. You enter through a courtyard cluttered with a collection of U.S. military equipment. Inside the museum, I moved down rows of grisly photographs intended to

demonstrate American "crimes of aggression." It was a gut-wrenching experience to be reminded of the ghastly acts we Americans committed in that war, but they were matched by the barbarisms and atrocities on the part of the North Vietnamese and Viet Cong.

The Vietnamese working at the War Relics Museum were all smiles and cordiality, an odd juxtaposition with the brutal tenor of the exhibit. Stranger still was the presence of a water puppet theater on

the grounds of the museum, as well as craft booths immediately outside the door of the main photo gallery. One instant I was perusing the horrific effects of napalm, Agent Orange, and white phosphorus, and the next I was browsing among lacquerware jewelry boxes and hand-carved statues of Buddha.

In a way, though, that disquieting combination sums up the nature of a visit to this country, where reminders of war coexist with examples of Vietnam's lasting heritage. Even for someone who comes here seeking to experience Vietnam for itself and not to wallow in the war, new sights inevitably trigger old associations. The trick, I discovered—not always an easy one—is to keep those memories from blinding us to the worth and beauty of what we're seeing now.

I returned to the Rex to pack up and settle my

Ironclad patrol boats of the U.S. Mobile Riverine Force prowl the slow-moving channels of the Mekong Delta in an effort to deny Viet Cong units sanctuary amid the 26,000-square-mile labyrinth of paddies, canals, and mangrove swamps.

In the Mekong Delta town of Phung Hiep, seven canals intersect to create one of Southeast Asia's most colorful and authentic floating markets. Formed from silt deposited by the mighty Mekong River, which begins in the faraway mountains of Tibet, the lush, board-flat southern delta is among Vietnam's most densely populated regions.

account. Afterward, Giang was waiting in the lobby to see me off. He stood by my side as the bellhop stored my bags in the taxi.

"Good-bye, Mr. Paul Martin," my young guide said as we shook hands.

"Good-bye, Giang. Thanks for everything. And good luck."

I meant that sincerely. I wished Giang and his countrymen all the luck possible, in healing the

Taking aim over the Mekong Delta, a door gunner of a U.S. Navy UH-1 Huey helicopter fires his M-60 machine gun at Viet Cong guerrillas in the U-Minh Forest, the world's largest mangrove swamp outside the Amazon and a VC stronghold throughout the war.

Vietnamese traders in boats of every size ply the Mekong Delta's endless waterways. Called the breadbasket of Vietnam, the delta grows enough rice to feed the country, plus help meet export demands. The region also produces citrus fruit, sugarcane, and coconuts, and many delta inhabitants have lately turned to lucrative fish farming.

wounds of their long struggle, in furthering the material progress of the past decade. Perhaps if I returned in another ten years I'd see an even more prosperous Vietnam, and maybe—wouldn't it be something—a Vietnam in which political freedoms had caught up with economic ones.

The taxi door slammed shut, and the car pulled away from the curb, leaving Giang alone in front of the Rex, a child of Hanoi waving at the departing American, a friendly smile on his face.

A few minutes later I was deep in the bedlam of Tan Son Nhat Airport, struggling with my two bags through a chattering throng of Vietnamese blocking the terminal entrance. Once I was inside, the check-in went smoothly, and soon I was past security and waiting in the second-floor departure lounge, where

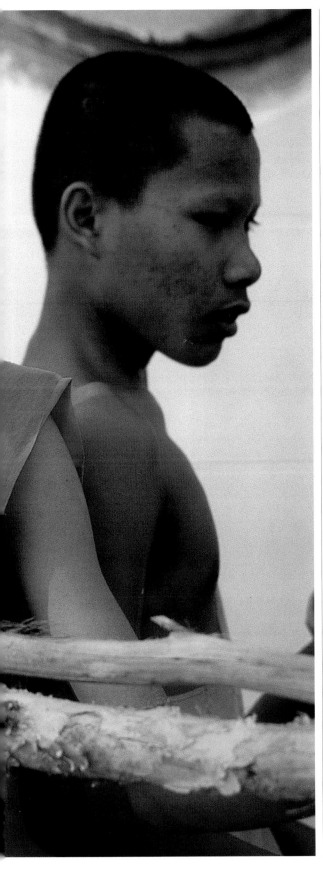

the picture windows gave a fine prospect of the airport. Across the tarmac stood rows of round-topped revetments that had once protected U.S. fighters from mortar attacks. They were empty now, forlorn and untended, their tops overtaken with fuzzy brown lichens. Down at one end of the terminal, several old warplanes had been herded together, remnants of the once mighty American arsenal—an elephants' graveyard of derelict C-130s and decrepit

Cobra helicopters with sagging rotors, as purposeless as a roomful of worn-out combat boots.

　　Then here came my arriving plane, taxiing up to the terminal—a gleaming white Boeing 767 with the distinctive blue stork emblem of Vietnam Airlines on its tail. On the first leg of my journey home, I would be flying in an American-made airliner bearing the logo of Communist Vietnam's official carrier. Suddenly something occurred to me—when I'd arrived in Hanoi, the Vietnam Airlines jet that I'd flown in on had been an Airbus, manufactured by the French-led European consortium.

　　If we couldn't beat them, we'd sell them airplanes. Clearly, the new offensive for Vietnam was underway, and this time around everyone could be winners.

Ministering to the Mekong Delta's sizable Khmer minority, Buddhist monks tend a monastery near Can Tho and dry rice at a temple near Soc Trang. The Khmer-speaking clergy are a tangible reminder that the delta was once part of the sprawling Cambodian kingdom that also included parts of Laos and Thailand.

Following pages: Harbinger of better times, an oil tanker rides at anchor off Vung Tau, an offshore-oil-drilling headquarters and beach resort southeast of Saigon on the South China Sea. Known to the French as Cap Saint Jacques, Vung Tau exemplifies the twin forces of business and tourism that are helping to shape the new Vietnam.

A Brief History of Vietnam

SOMETIME between 200 B.C. and A.D. 200, the intermingling of the Red River Delta's early inhabitants resulted in a distinct Vietnamese people. Virtually from the outset, the Vietnamese were ruled by the Chinese, and they would continue to be until A.D. 938.

During the centuries of Chinese control over the Red River Delta, two independent states rose to power in what is now central and southern Vietnam. From the first to the sixth centuries, the kingdom of Funan held sway over the Mekong Delta and the region that is now Cambodia; the kingdom was overthrown by the Mon-Khmer, who founded the Cambodian empire.

Along the coast of central Vietnam, the kingdom of Champa ruled from the late second century until the 15th, when it was conquered by the Vietnamese, who expanded steadily southward after expelling the Chinese. In the 17th and early 18th centuries, the Vietnamese would wrest the Mekong Delta from Cambodia, essentially completing the formation of their country.

Of the more than a dozen dynasties that have ruled independent Vietnam, three are considered "great." The first was the Ly (1009-1225), whose rulers established Hanoi as their capital in the year 1010, naming it Thang Long, the City of the Soaring Dragon. (It was not until 1831 that the name Hanoi—City in a Bend of the River—came into use.) The Ly built new roads, dikes, and canals, and they vigorously promoted agriculture. In 1044—22 years before William the Conqueror invaded England—the Ly founded Vietnam's first postal service.

The Ly dynasty ended in overthrow by the Tran, who established the second great dynasty (1225-1400). In 1407, the Chinese reconquered Vietnam, but this time their rule

lasted only two decades. In 1428, they were driven out by the Vietnamese hero who established the third great dynasty, Le Loi. The Le dynasty, which held power until 1524, introduced a series of remarkable reforms. Art, literature, and education were promoted. Large landowners were forced to distribute their holdings to the landless. Legal reforms gave women nearly equal rights with men.

In the 17th and 18th centuries, Vietnam was split by warring factions. Northern Vietnam was ruled by the powerful Trinh lords, the south controlled by lords of the Nguyen line. In 1786, three brothers, the Tay Son, briefly reunited the country, but even as they fought to depose the Trinh and Nguyen lords, their empire began fragmenting.

In 1802, one of the Nguyen lords defeated the Tay Son and proclaimed himself Emperor Gia Long, establishing the last of Vietnam's dynasties. The Nguyen made Hue their imperial capital, and they ruled from there until the last Vietnamese emperor, Bao Dai, abdicated to a delegation representing Ho Chi Minh in 1945.

Vietnam's contacts with the West began as early as A.D. 166, when Roman travelers passed through the Red River Delta. It wasn't until much later, however, that there was any sustained Western contact. By 1516, a number of Portuguese adventurers had arrived, followed by missionaries and soldiers. Over the next century a trading center and mission were established in the port of Faifo, just south of present-day Danang. The Portuguese were followed by missionaries from Spain, Italy, and France. Everyone seemed intent on converting the Vietnamese, and in the process, cultivating stronger trading ties, but no one had much luck in making a profit from trade with the Vietnamese. The Dutch tried and failed, as did the English.

The early French trading efforts foundered as well, but the French never gave up. Off and on for nearly two centuries, the French kept lurking around Indochina. From about the 1850s on, France abandoned diplomatic overtures and settled on a policy of conquest. It would take them several decades, but by 1893 they had carved out an Indochinese empire that included Vietnam, Laos, and Cambodia. The French then set about plundering the immense natural wealth of those holdings.

The exploitation visited on the Vietnamese by their French masters created fertile conditions for the resistance movements that sprang up over the years. Most of the resistance efforts were successfully put down, but in 1925 a new movement was established by a man calling himself Nguyen Ai Quoc, who in later years would take the name Ho Chi Minh, the Bringer of Light. Ho's Vietnam Revolutionary Youth League became the nucleus of the Vietnamese Communist Party. In World War II, Ho formed the League for the Independence of Vietnam, or Viet Minh, which, during its resistance to the Japanese occupation of Vietnam, received money and arms from the United States through the O.S.S.

The American support of the Viet Minh led Ho to believe that the United States would back his bid for an independent Vietnam. But after the war, the Allies allowed France to reoccupy Indochina, setting the stage for the protracted guerrilla campaign that resulted in France's ouster in 1954 and the subsequent partitioning of Vietnam into North and South. The recognition and support of South Vietnam by the United States would lead to the bloody conflict that ended in 1975 when the Communists overran Saigon, proclaiming an independent Socialist Republic of Vietnam.

Chronology

208 B.C. – Breakaway Chinese general Trieu Da conquers proto-Vietnamese and establishes kingdom of Nam Viet; empire eventually extends from the Red River Delta as far south as present-day Danang.

111 B.C. – China's Han dynasty emperor Wu Ti conquers Nam Viet empire.

A.D. 40-43 – First major Vietnamese rebellion against Chinese rule led by two of Vietnam's greatest heroes, the Trung Sisters, who drown themselves rather than surrender when their revolt is put down.

166 – Roman travelers pass through Red River Delta; first known contact with West.

938 – Vietnamese forces led by Ngo Quyen defeat Chinese armies, ending China's millennium-long rule.

939-965 – Ngo dynasty rules the independent state of Vietnam.

968-980 – Dinh dynasty

980-1009 – Early Le dynasty

1009-1225 – Ly dynasty, first of Vietnam's three great dynasties

1225-1400 – Tran dynasty, second great dynasty

1400-1407 – Ho dynasty

1407-1427 – China regains control of Vietnam.

1428 – Chinese defeated by Vietnamese hero Le Loi.

1428-1524 – Later Le dynasty, the country's third great dynasty

Late 15th century – Kingdom of Champa overrun (present-day central Vietnam).

Early 16th century – Portuguese establish trading mission in port of Faifo (present-day Hoi An).

1527-1592 – Mac dynasty

17th-18th centuries – Vietnam divided; Trinh lords rule in north, Nguyen lords in south.

17th-early 18th centuries – Control of Mekong Delta wrested from Cambodia.

1786-1802 – Tay Son Rebels control country.

1802 – Tay Sons defeated by Nguyen Anh, who proclaims himself Emperor Gia Long and establishes final Vietnamese dynasty.

1802-1945 – Nguyen dynasty

1850s – France embarks on policy of conquest in Indochina.

1883 – France establishes protectorate over the northern and central regions of Vietnam (Tonkin and Annam) and rules the southern region (Cochinchina) as a colony, effectively controlling entire country.

1893 – France consolidates rule over Vietnam, Laos, and Cambodia in so-called Indochinese Union.

1940 – Japan occupies Indochina during World War II.

1941 – Ho Chi Minh returns to Vietnam after 30 years of exile and forms Viet Minh to fight French and Japanese.

July-Aug. 1945 – Potsdam Conference permits French to reoccupy Indochina after World War II.

Aug. 23, 1945 – Last Vietnamese emperor, Bao Dai, abdicates in favor of Viet Minh.

Sept. 2, 1945 – Ho Chi Minh proclaims an independent Democratic Republic of Vietnam.

1946-1954 – Franco-Viet Minh War

May 7, 1954 – French suffer catastrophic defeat at Dien Bien Phu.

July 1954 – Geneva Accords negotiate end to Indochina conflict and call for partitioning of Vietnam and nationwide elections in July 1956.

1955 – Southern ruler Ngo Dinh Diem refuses to participate in nationwide elections; holds referendum on his continued rule, afterward declaring himself president of new Republic of Vietnam (South Vietnam); U.S. immediately recognizes new government and closes its consulate in Hanoi.

1959 – North Vietnam steps up campaign to liberate the south, setting stage for the Vietnam War; first American troops to die in Vietnam killed at Bien Hoa.

1961-1963 – Kennedy administration increases U.S. military advisors to more than 15,000.

Aug. 7, 1964 – Tonkin Gulf Resolution paves the way for Johnson administration's escalation of U.S. military role in Vietnam.

Mar. 8, 1965 – First U.S. combat troops land at Danang.

Jan.-Feb. 1968 – Communist Tet Offensive undermines American public support for U.S. involvement in war.

April 1969 – U.S. troop deployment peaks at 543,000.

June 1969 – President Nixon begins American troop withdrawals.

Mar. 29, 1973 – Last American troops leave Vietnam; during war's course, 3.1 million Americans serve in Vietnam.

April 30, 1975 – Fall of Saigon brings end to the war and reunification of Vietnam. Final estimates of casualties: 58,000 Americans killed or missing; 880,000-1,100,000 Vietnamese soldiers killed, 300,000 missing; 315,000-2,000,000 Vietnamese civilians killed. (Vietnamese totals represent combined figures for North and South; ranges reflect discrepancies between U.S. and Vietnamese estimates.)

Dec. 25, 1978 – Vietnam invades Cambodia in response to repeated attacks by Khmer Rouge on Vietnamese border villages.

Feb. 1979 – China invades Vietnam in response to persecution of ethnic-Chinese and the attack on China's Cambodian allies, the Khmer Rouge; Chinese forces withdraw after 17 days.

Dec. 1986 – Economic liberalization policy— *doi moi*—announced; allows free-market competition.

Sept. 1989 – Vietnam withdraws from Cambodia.

1991 – Soviet economic aid to Vietnam ends.

Feb. 1994 – U.S. lifts 19-year trade embargo against Vietnam.

July 1995 – U.S. and Vietnam reestablish diplomatic relations.

Bibliography

Andrews, Owen D.; Elliott, Douglas; and Levin, Laurence L. *Vietnam: Images from Combat Photographers.* Washington, D.C.: Starwood Publishing, 1991.

Cohen, Barbara. *The Vietnam Guidebook.* 3rd ed. New York: Houghton Mifflin Company, 1994.

Currey, Cecil B. *Victory at Any Cost: The Genius of Viet Nam's Gen. Vo Nguyen Giap.* Washington, D.C.: Brassey's Inc., 1997.

Dougan, Clark, and Weiss, Stephen. *The American Experience in Vietnam.* Boston: Boston Publishing Company, 1988.

Fox, Diane Niblack, and Taylor, Nora A. *Van Mieu Quoc Tu Giam: The Temple of Literature.* Hanoi, Vietnam: Gioi Publishers, 1994.

Hiebert, Murray. *Vietnam Notebook.* Hong Kong: Review Publishing, 1993.

Isaacs, Arnold. *Without Honor: Defeat in Vietnam and Cambodia.* Baltimore: Johns Hopkins University Press, 1983.

Karnow, Stanley. *Vietnam: A History.* 2nd ed. New York: Viking, 1991.

Ly Van Sau; Dalby, Stewart; Vo Nguyen Giap; Bui Van Tung; Bui Quang Than. "Saigon: April 30, 1975" (accounts of the fall of Saigon). *Vietnam Economic Times,* April 1995: 40-45.

Meyerson, Joel D. *Images of a Lengthy War: The United States Army in Vietnam.* Washington, D.C.: Center of Military History, United States Army, 1986.

Nguyen Dac Xuan. *A Guide for the Citadel of Hue.* Translated by Nghi Huan. 2nd ed. Hue, Vietnam: Thuan Hoa Publishing House, 1994.

Olson, James, ed. *Dictionary of the Vietnam War.* New York: Peter Bedrick Books, 1988.

Quang Nam-Da Nang Culture and Information Service. *Museum of Cham Sculpture in Da Nang.* Hanoi, Vietnam: Foreign Languages Publishing House, 1987.

SarDesai, D.R. *Southeast Asia: Past & Present.* 3rd ed. Boulder, Colorado: Westview Press, 1994.

Sheehan, Neil. *After the War Was Over: Hanoi and Saigon.* New York: Random House, 1992.

Storey, Robert, and Robinson, Daniel. *Vietnam: a Lonely Planet travel survival kit.* 2nd ed. Hawthorn, Australia: Lonely Planet, 1995.

Summers, Harry G., Jr. *On Strategy: A Critical Analysis of the Vietnam War.* New York: Dell, 1982.

Summers, Harry G., Jr. *Vietnam War Almanac.* New York: Facts on File Publications, 1985.

Unsigned article. "FYI: Financial Statistics" (review of Vietnam's 1996 demographic and financial statistics). *The Vietnam Business Journal,* Jan./Feb. 1997: 16.

CHINA

Ha Giang

Cao Bang

Fan Si Pan
Lao Cai
Sa Pa
Lai Chau

Lang Son
Thai Nguyen

Yen Bai

Hong (Red)

Da (Black)

Dien Bien Phu
Son La

Hanoi

NATIONAL HIGHWAY

Bai Chay

Haiphong

Cuc Phuong National Park

Nam Dinh

Halong Bay

Cat Ba National Park

Red River Delta

Thanh Hoa

GULF OF TONKIN

Hainan (CHINA)

Elongated, mountainous nation stretches some one thousand miles north to south, knit together by National Highway 1, which runs from the China border in the north to deep in the Mekong Delta.

Vinh

Viangchan (Vientiane)

CHINA
MYANMAR
VIETNAM
THAILAND
LAOS
PHILIPPINES
CAMBODIA
MALAYSIA
Singapore
INDONESIA

Mekong

Dong Hoi

Former DMZ

Dong Ha
Quang Tri
Hue

Khe Sanh

Royal Tombs

Danang

China Beach
Hoi An

My Son Cham Temples

Marble Mountains

Quang Ngai

Dak To

Kontum

Pleiku

Qui Nhon

Railroad
0   100
Kilometers
0   100
Miles

CAMBODIA

CENTRAL HIGHLANDS

Mekong

Ban Me Thuot

Nha Trang
Cam Ranh

Dalat

Phnom Penh

Tay Ninh

Cu Chi Tunnels

Bien Hoa

NATIONAL HIGHWAY

Ho Chi Minh City (Saigon)

My Tho

Vung Tau

Can Tho

SOUTH CHINA SEA

GULF OF THAILAND

Mekong River Delta

Ca Mau

Index

Index

Index

Page numbers in bold indicate illustrations.
Page numbers in italic indicate references in caption.

Index

Index

Biographical Notes

PAUL MARTIN began his writing career in 1968 as a U.S. Navy journalist after receiving a B.A. in English from Central Missouri State University. In 1970-71, he was stationed in Vietnam, covering American and South Vietnamese naval activities. Following his service, he earned an M.A. in journalism at the University of Missouri, and for the next six years he was managing editor of the monthly medical journal *Continuing Education for the Family Physician.* In 1979, Martin joined the staff of the National Geographic Society, where he has been an editor of *World* magazine and written or edited over a dozen books. Since 1989, Martin has been managing editor of *National Geographic Traveler,* four-time winner of the *Folio:* Editorial Excellence Award for best travel magazine. He has contributed articles on Cuba, Jamaica, Vietnam, and many other destinations.

STEVE RAYMER, a *National Geographic* magazine photographer for more than two decades, is a professor of journalism at Indiana University in Bloomington. He is also on the faculty of the University's Russian and East European Institute. Raymer earned B.S. and M.A. degrees at the University of Wisconsin-Madison and studied Soviet and Russian affairs at Stanford University as a John S. Knight Journalism Fellow. As an Army public affairs officer from 1967 to 1969, Raymer escorted correspondents covering the Vietnam War. He joined the staff of *National Geographic* in 1972, launching a career that has taken him to more than 80 countries. From famines in Bangladesh and Ethiopia to the collapse of the Soviet Union, Raymer's photographs have illustrated some 30 *National Geographic* articles and numerous Society books. Raymer was named Magazine Photographer of the Year in 1976 by the National Press Photographers Association and received a citation for excellence in foreign reporting from the Overseas Press Club in 1981. He is a four time first-prize winner of the White House News Photographers' Association photo contest.

About Gates & Bridges

Gates as in gates to new worlds
to more knowledge
to better understanding
to more tolerance

Bridges as in bridges between cultures,
continents, people,
past, present and
future generations.